RECRUITMENT WORKBOOK

RECRUITMENT WORKBOOK

STAN CRABTREE

KOGAN PAGE

First published in 1991

Kogan Page Limited
120 Pentonville Road
London N1 9JN

British Library Cataloguing in Publication Data
A CIP record for this book is available from the British Library.

ISBN 0-7494-0110-9

Typeset by DP Photosetting, Aylesbury, Bucks
Printed and bound in Great Britain by
Biddles Limited, Guildford and King's Lynn

◀ CONTENTS ▶

◀ RECRUITMENT PROGRAMME AT A GLANCE ▶

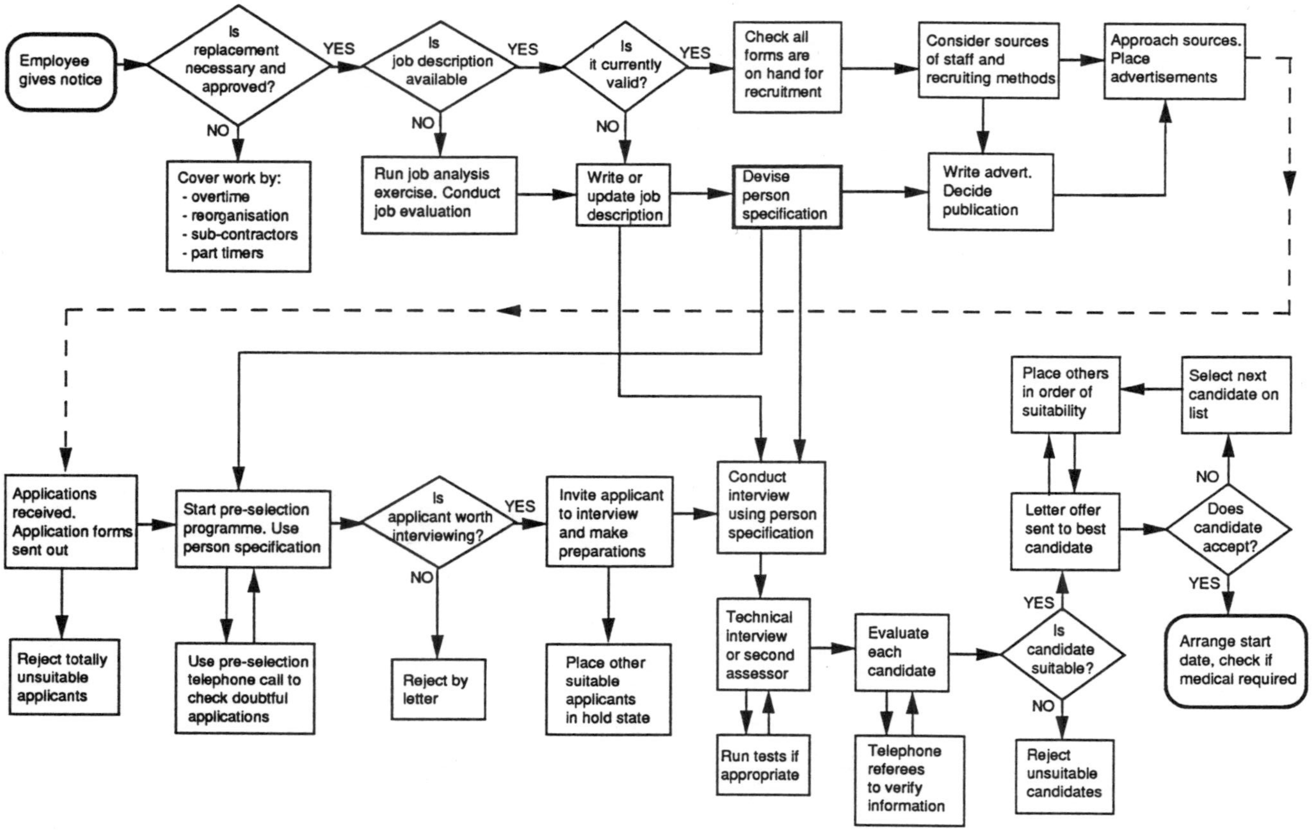

◀ INTRODUCTION ▶

To have an efficient, stable and contented workforce in a small or medium-sized organisation today, a well-thought out recruitment policy is essential. Get it wrong and the repercussions can be far-reaching. You not only have a disillusioned, disappointed employee, but the discontent can spread through a department. Time, money and effort spent in training and establishing a worker in his/her role are lost overnight. The overall cost, considering that the process has to start all over again, is considerable.

Responsibility for recruitment is an unenviable task. The recruiter not only has to assess the technical capability of an aspiring applicant but also judge if he/she will be compatible in a new environment and acceptable to the existing staff. Nowadays, with an ever-increasing number of the population seeking to get back to gainful employment and leave the ranks of the unemployed, the recruiter has the added burden of thinking for the candidate. The applicant facing you across the table may be so anxious to obtain work that the suitability of the job for them is disregarded. The final decision and responsibility rests with you, the recruiter.

The interview is arguably the best medium by which you can discover something about an applicant's suitability for a particular job. Many question its value but at least there is personal communication. You come face to face with the applicant, which has to be better than contact by letter or even the telephone. You may feel that you are a good judge of character and able to sum up the person opposite after just a few minutes. But can you? Human nature is often unpredictable and indeterminable. And you often have less than an hour in which to form an opinion. In the end you may rely on a gut feeling to help you decide whether the face across the table really matches the person specification you have drawn up.

That is where this workbook comes into play. It describes each stage of a recruitment programme and indicates the most important aspects of this operation. Whether it is a single vacancy to be filled or a group of vacancies, a junior clerk or a departmental head, following the procedure outlined in this book will, we hope, make the process straightforward and trouble free.

Chapter 1 poses the question: Do I need to recruit at all? It summarises the options that should be considered before engaging new staff. Chapter 2 helps you to avoid certain problems by describing the constraints of current legislation and how they can affect elements of the recruiting process. Without this knowledge you may inadvertently find yourself accused of discrimination!

The need to analyse the routine work operation and draw up job descriptions and person specifications is covered in Chapter 3. Chapter 4 prepares you for recruitment by listing what you need in the way of forms and other information to carry you through the programme. Chapter 5 lists and comments on the various sources of staff at all levels. It helps you to decide which method of recruitment will be most suitable for you.

You start in earnest once the applications start coming in. Preselection is essential and Chapter 6 shows you the proved methods to do this as efficiently as possible. Once your shortlist of candidates is drawn up you are ready to start interviewing the prospects. We do not provide lists of hypothetical questions to remember, but Chapter 7 more especially makes you aware of the important principles of interviewing and emphasises the use of a systematic routine when facing your applicant across the table.

You're now on the home run. Chapter 8 spells out the methods by which you are able to make your final selection. In conclusion, Chapter 9 advises on the final stages of the recruiting campaign.

The book contains many examples of forms and letters. With minor changes you can use any of these in your recruiting operation and thus save yourself hours of brain-work. In addition, throughout the text we continually stress the right way to do things as recommended by the Institute of Personnel Management. Apart from extending courtesy to all applicants it enhances the image of your firm.

The selection and recruitment of staff may be regarded as a nuisance by busy managers who feel their main function is to run the business and maximise profitability. But labour resources must be placed high on the list of contributing factors that attain that profitability and a serious approach to recruitment is thus of vital importance. It is hoped that the *Recruitment Workbook* will help to make the manager's task in this operation just that little bit easier.

◀ CHAPTER 1 ▶

NEED TO RECRUIT

The title of this opening chapter may appear simplistic but it does need some consideration.

Is recruitment necessary? Consider the hidden expenses of labour.

Recruitment can be expensive and labour costs are not confined to wages. There is the hidden expense of office accommodation, car parking space, social and safety services and facilities, pension payments, National Insurance contributions and any perks or benefits to name only the obvious. Research has shown that the total cost is twice the salary paid - more for senior management and specialists. These costs start from the commencement date and continue irrespective of the gaps in productivity caused by holidays, training, sickness and other planned or unplanned absences. In addition, there is the recruitment responsibility of getting it right! A hired employee who leaves for whatever reason after a few months escalates the overall cost.

Engagement of any worker should therefore not be gone into lightly or without some thought and consideration of the possibilities of other means of satisfying the need for work support.

Whether or not there is an alternative means of avoiding engaging new staff will depend upon how long the demand will last and the amount or intensity of the labour shortfall. With a heavy and prolonged requirement there may be no alternative to recruitment. But consideration should be given to the following solutions for situations where it appears that the demand will not reach this level.

An objective evaluation is essential before any decision is made.

Overview

- Have you as, say, a divisional manager been given all the facts of future company policy?
- Are there any changes planned to the present work schedule that could mean that the replacement of current shortages are unnecessary? Perhaps the jobs would eventually become obsolete anyway.
- Another point to ponder is the present rate of output. Would it be disastrous if production were to fall by 10 per cent? If the area of staff shortage is a section in a chain of operations, each dependent upon a supply from an earlier source, this may not be practicable but, where the final product is contained and seen as one operation, a minor fall in output and subsequent short delay in deliveries to customers may be acceptable. This path is certainly worth considering where the effect is known to be seasonal or of an unpredictable length of time.

Overtime may provide a temporary solution.

Overtime

Overtime by existing staff is perhaps the first remedy that springs to mind. If it is not in their terms of employment some staff will not entertain this at all. But there could be a few who will welcome it, especially if it is not on a permanent basis. It could well suffice for seasonal demands and for periods when some staff are on holiday. Continuous overtime borne by a few is not to be recommended. Irrespective of the monetary gain the incumbent often becomes frustrated and resentful when the novelty wears off. It must also be carefully monitored and controlled from the outset. It should never be seen as a permanent solution to what could materialise as a long-term shortage of labour.

Reorganisation may avoid the need to recruit.

Reorganisation

After analysis it might be possible to reorganise the staff to make good the labour deficit. If the type of work has grown in an unexpected quarter it may be possible to transfer certain tasks to another area where there is a surplus of staff time. This can often be a painless exercise when it is undertaken in a mechanised discipline; for example, the redistribution of certain computer or data entry functions to an operator in a different department.

This can extend beyond departments and divisions in the larger firm.

Redundancy of labour being considered in one section may be avoided by redeploying the worker in another phase of operations. This is usually to be preferred even if some retraining is necessary. Thus there is always a need for good communication between department heads to ensure that recruitment (and redundancy) do not take place inadvertently.

Can redundant labour be redeployed if retrained?

Is it possible to mechanise certain sedentary jobs of a clerical or accountancy nature? This may mean expanding existing computer networks and considering new software. But the gain will be long term and add to the overall efficiency of the discipline that is computerised. Many small go-ahead companies (and sections of the public corporate sector) have now almost eliminated secretarial support. Their staff - often up to middle management level - input their own correspondence on a personal computer. Word-processing techniques make a professional appearance in letters relatively easy to achieve.

Can jobs be mechanised?

Shift working

Shift working opens the way to phasing in part-time work, job sharing and temporary workers.

For a serious ongoing shortage of manpower the introduction of shift working should be considered - even if it means extending the present times of coverage by only a few hours.

Seven am to nine pm can be conveniently split into two, seven-hour sessions. Further, once established, this leaves the way open to phase in part-time working, job sharing and also temporary workers. However, the introduction of shifts could be a big exercise. It should never be taken lightly as there may be other aspects to be examined or reviewed.

- Maintenance and durability of machines and equipment must be considered.
- Shift work requires co-operation and acceptance by the workforce who will be expected to work the revised hours.
- New terms or contracts of employment will inevitably have to be drawn up and the question of increased rates owing to the working of shifts or unsocial hours considered.

Prior sounding out and discussions with the staff are prerequisite to an operation such as this.

Can some of the work be relocated?

Sub-contractors

Where the problem of staff is not expected to be long term, sub-contractors may be used provided the required skills are available in this type of workforce. This avoids the administration of individual members of an irregular part-time or temporary workforce. Some of the work may lend itself to being moved to a different location. A certain amount of control is obviously lost by using this method but is often matched by the gain in overall flexibility. By inserting suitable clauses you are able to end the contractual agreement if it is seen not to be working out. The track record of contractors tendering or being sought to undertake the work should bc ascertained from a reliable source before serious commitments are made.

Use of specialist agencies.

Agencies

How the additional work is to be done necessarily depends upon the type of work and the skills required. For clerical positions, an agency is perhaps the best course. In most cases they perform the same function as sub-contractors with the administrative tasks included. You, as user, simply pay an hourly rate for the work. There are now agencies which specialise in specific areas of work; for example, accountancy, hotel and catering, nursing, as well as the more common secretarial and word-processing functions. The length of time of the requirement should be made known at the outset and the rate of pay negotiated accordingly. Remember that by using sub-contracted or agency staff, although the expense may appear significant, you are avoiding the hidden costs mentioned at the beginning of the chapter.

Part-time workers

Potential workforce in waiting.

There is a large potential workforce of clerical and secretarial staff just waiting for part-time opportunities in all areas. Many register at the local Job Centre. Advertising in the press is another way of attracting staff. A short classified advertisement in the local free newspaper will always produce a response from a number of enthusiastic workers only too pleased to help out. Don't dismiss support from that often neglected section of the community – the retired (or nowadays, possibly the early retired). Here is a source of labour – skilled, willing and usually of the highest integrity.

In these circumstances you would be well advised to come to some private arrangement with prospective workers. Remember, there are National Insurance and Inland Revenue collections to be made for a certain minimum number of hours and payments in a week. Details are given in NI information sheets issued to firms already operating PAYE.

◀ CHAPTER 2 ▶

THE LEGAL SIDE

The recruiter's aim is to select the best applicant for the job and this will normally be done irrespective of sex, race or any disabilities. In general, common sense should prevail and the manager will be able to carry out the selection exercise without any problems. However, situations can arise where failed applicants feel they were unsuccessful for reasons other than technical unsuitability. The manager must be able to recognise a delicate problem before it reaches an unmanageable level. We can only touch briefly on the matter here but all staff responsible for recruitment would be well advised to go a little deeper into the legal side of the subject.

Main Acts of Parliament.

Parliamentary Acts of note are:

- The Race Relations Act (1976)
- The Sex Discrimination Act (1975)
- The Equal Pay Act (1970)
- The Disabled Persons (Employment) Act (1944 and 1958)
- The Rehabilitation of Offenders Act (1974)
- Employment Act (1990).

Each has an associated Code of Practice which sets out how the Act is to be interpreted and enforced.

Race Relations Act (1976)

The basic requirements were covered in the Act of 1968. They refer to discrimination of colour, race, nationality or ethnic or national origin against people in, or applying for, employment. Discriminatory actions against the above mentioned categories are defined as:

Discriminatory actions - they can be unintentional.

- refusing work to a qualified person;
- not offering the same terms and conditions of employment enjoyed by other staff because of colour, race, nationality or ethnic or national origin;
- not making available training, and not offering the promotion available to other staff employed in the same circumstances.

The discrimination does not have to be intentional; indeed, it could happen in all innocence. If any of the employer's actions are capable of being seen as fitting into one of the above definitions, the firm will be guilty of exercising discrimination.

Segregation on racial grounds.

The Act specifies that it is unlawful to segregate employees on racial grounds. Making separate arrangements for people of different racial groups is classed as treating those people less favourably and therefore committing direct discrimination.

Legislation also ensures that people who give evidence or information against persons making the discrimination are protected. They must not be victimised or in any way treated less favourably than others. Where victimisation is proved the persons committing such actions would be guilty of an offence.

The Commission for Racial Equality.

The Commission for Racial Equality was set up as part of the current 1976 Act and replaced the earlier Race Relations Board. It carries much more power and reinforces certain shortcomings in the earlier Act. The aim of the Commission was to eliminate racial discrimination, a task which it has unfortunately found to be fraught with difficulty. In 1984 the Commission published a new Code of Practice which concentrated on the promotion of equality of opportunity in all areas of employment. Although not law, the provisions can be used in evidence to support claimants at any industrial tribunal.

Powers of an industrial tribunal.

A tribunal has no legal right to force an employer to offer a position to a person who may have been discriminated against. However, if there is sufficient evidence to show that discrimination has taken place an order can be made to the company to rectify the matter. In addition, the tribunal has the power to award damages for hurt feelings, even where there is no financial loss.

The Code of Practice specifically recommends that:

- an equal opportunities policy should be implemented by employers and be the responsibility of a member of senior management;
- efforts should be made to ensure that all employees are made aware of this policy and its implications;
- line managers and supervisory staff should undergo training and have guidance to ensure that their position in law is known and understood.

Recording new employees' race or ethnic origin.

A useful practice is to ascertain and record a new employee's race or ethnic origin on engagement. To do this, a form stating that the company operates an equal opportunities policy which ensures that all its staff (management and shop floor) do not discriminate against any person is presented to the new starter. He/she ticks an appropriate box as either 'male' or 'female' and defines his/her ethnic origin (which could include UK European). The form could be set out as a letter and include a qualifying statement advising that its completion will assist in the monitoring of the company policy and an assurance that the details given will only be used for this purpose. It is useful if this form is completed during an informal meeting on the new entrant's first day at work when the line manager can explain its purpose. An example of a typical layout for this purpose is shown on page 23.

Recruitment advertising.

The effect of race relations legislation extends to advertising. To publish a job advertisement which appears to discriminate on racial grounds is unlawful; and any illustration featuring characters should ideally show a male and female.

As mentioned earlier, an unsuccessful applicant may feel he was discriminated against simply because he did not get the job. At the time it may have been obvious to the manager that another candidate was much more suitable for the position and his selection will have been based on evidence to support this. But will he remember the circumstances a few months later when his decision is challenged? Because of this possibility it is essential that some written documentation is available to support his decision if required by tribunal officials. The notes taken during or immediately after an interview will be useful in these circumstances and they should be sufficiently comprehensive to justify the final selection.

Offending questions referring to race.

Questions during an interview should be chosen with care. For example, the following questions are an invitation to an unsuccessful applicant to claim racial discrimination.

Sex and ethnic origin monitoring

Dear ....

The Acme Trading Company is an equal opportunities employer and does not discriminate against any person on the grounds of sex, race or ethnic origin.

Following recommendations of the Commission for Racial Equality (set up as part of the Race Relations Act 1976) the Acme Trading Company maintains records of new entrants' sex and ethnic origin to assist in the monitoring of the above policy.

Please supply information by ticking the appropriate box below. The information provided will not be used for any purpose other than that explained above.

MALE	☐	FEMALE	☐

EUROPEAN	☐	AFRICAN	☐
ASIAN	☐	OTHER	☐
AFRO-CARIBBEAN	☐	(specify)	....

SURNAME ....   FORENAME(S) ....

DATE ....

- 'Have you had any trouble with white workers?'
- 'How long do you expect to stay in the country?'
- 'Being Irish, are you inclined to lose your temper when annoyed?'
- 'Have you had any problems in dealing with members of the public?' (the implication being because the applicant is black).

Sex Discrimination Act (1975)

This law refers to discrimination against women in employment and makes it unlawful to discriminate on grounds of sex or marital status. It became law in December 1975 at the same time as the Equal Pay Act (1970).

Can apply to men as well as women.

Most of the Act's clauses refer to discrimination against women by treating them less favourably than men. However, it should be realised that under the Act, when circumstances demand it, men have equal protection against discrimination on the grounds of sex.

The Sex Discrimination Act applies to recruitment of new staff and opportunities for training or promotion of existing staff. Complaints are initially considered by the Advisory, Conciliation and Arbitration Service (ACAS). If a matter cannot be resolved it goes to an industrial tribunal which has the power to order a particular course of action or award compensation.

The Equal Opportunities Commission was established by the Sex Discrimination Act in order to enforce the Act's rulings. Its prime function is to:

- investigate and remedy discrimination on the grounds of sex or marital status;
- promote equal opportunities for men and women;
- monitor the implementation of the Sex Discrimination Act and also the Equal Pay Act.

Role of Equal Opportunities Commission.

The Commission must educate the public in the implications of the Act and influence public opinion. It also imposes the Act's rulings by the issue of 'non-discriminatory notices' which are enforceable in a civil court of law. In their own interest, all firms should think seriously about implementing an equal opportunities policy. Such a policy should make sure that every staff member is treated fairly at work and every applicant for a job is given an equal chance of employment. It means that they should be assessed according to their capability to perform a job to the exclusion of all other considerations.

The same legislation on victimisation applies under the Sex Discrimination Act as that defined for the Race Relations Act.

Sex discrimination in advertising.

Constraints on the recruiting process include advertising and interviewing. Care must be taken that these operations are not sexist or discriminatory. For example, the expression 'chairman' when used in advertising should be qualified by 'men or women may apply' and any illustrations in the advertisement should depict men and women equally. Tests used in a selection process should not be discriminatory.

The Sex Discrimination Act (1986) revised and added new aspects to the earlier Act. In particular it removed certain restrictions on hours of work by women and made some progress in equalising the age of retirement for women to that for men.

Offending questions on sex discrimination.

During the recruiting process, interviewers should take care not to introduce any question or observation that could be construed as discriminating against one sex. For example, some questions to avoid during an interview with a woman would be:

- 'Are you expecting to start a family in the near future?'
- 'What arrangements will you make for the children when you're on evening shift?'
- 'Do you see any problem with males working under you?'
- 'Is your husband liable to move with his job?'

Although possibly appearing quite reasonable to the interviewer this type of question could leave him/her open to an accusation of sex discrimination if for any reason the female applicant did not get the job.

Equal Pay Act (1970)

This was the first legislation promoting equality for women. Although dated 1970, it was only fully ratified in December 1975 and coincided with the promulgation of the Sex Discrimination Act. It has since been amended by the Equal Pay (Amended) Regulations (1983).

Requirements of Equal Pay Act.

The Equal Pay Act has three main sections and requirements:

- pay to be equal when a woman's work is of equal value and broadly similar to a man's;

- when evaluating a job, the same criteria must be used when analysing work done by men and women;
- any collective agreement containing discriminatory clauses may be reported to the Central Arbitration Board which has the power to amend them.

Dispensations which permit discrimination.

Genuine occupational qualifications

In some circumstances dispensations may be allowed from the Racial Discrimination Act and the Sex Discrimination Act. Dispensation allows certain aspects of sex discrimination but not marriage discrimination.

The Equal Opportunities Commission decided that certain exceptions under the Act can be claimed by an employer to recruit persons of a particular sex or racial group when:

- authenticity justifies the discrimination; for example, a Chinese waiter in a Chinese restaurant;
- welfare services are provided for a certain ethnic group in the form of a social worker for that particular group;
- a woman or man is required as an attendant in a respective ladies' or gentlemen's lavatory;
- it is impractical to provide separate sanitary or sleeping facilities – as in the case of, say, a small offshore drilling rig.

A further example might be where a Sikh is unable to obtain a post as a food preparer in a hotel kitchen owing to a ban on beards on the grounds of hygiene.

Reserved occupations.

Disabled Persons (Employment) Act (1958)

This Act together with its forerunner, the 1944 Act, is the main legislation for the employment of disabled people. Disabled people are defined as suffering some physical or mental impediment on a permanent basis. In the original 1944 Act, there were two jobs designated as reserved occupations for registered disabled people: car park attendants and operators of passenger lifts.

Additional provisions to 1958 Act.

Additions to the 1958 Act were made in 1980 and current legislation provides for the following:

- rehabilitation of disabled people at employment rehabilitation centres
- retraining of disabled people
- a register of disabled people
- a quota scheme.

Quota scheme.

The quota scheme applies to all firms where more than 20 staff are employed. In these cases registered disabled persons should account for at least 3 per cent of the total workforce. A point worth remembering by a manager about to recruit is that no non-disabled people should be recruited until the above quota is reached. It is therefore important (and a legal requirement) that an employer must keep records of the number of disabled persons employed at any time.

Code of Good Practice.

In 1984, the Manpower Services Commission produced a Code of Good Practice on the Employment of Disabled People.

Grants for firms and individuals.

Financial help in the form of grants may be obtained by firms for the employment of disabled people. A cash grant can be paid for adapting premises to accommodate a registered disabled person; for example, to meet safety requirements. Financial assistance in the event of travelling difficulties, cash towards the training of disabled people you hope to recruit and also the retraining of existing workers who have become disabled is available. Full details of these and the recruitment of disabled workers can be obtained from the Disablement Resettlement Officer at your local Job Centre.

Rehabilitation of Offenders Act (1974)

After certain lengths of time, people who have been convicted of an offence may omit to give details on an application form or CV and also during an interview. The individual is considered to be rehabilitated.

Expended convictions.

The periods when the sentence or fine is considered expendable vary from five years in the case of a fine, to ten years where a term of imprisonment of up to 30 months has been served. Dismissal from HM Services may be considered expended in seven years.

It is an offence for a prospective employer to consider offences committed by a person when that person has been rehabilitated. Further, an employer is not allowed to disclose the earlier conviction of a rehabilitated person in a reference (assuming he knows of such an offence). If disclosed, it must not be done with malice – to do so could involve the writer in accusations of defamation, irrespective of the truth of any information revealed.

Employment Act (1990)

This legislation, which refers to trade union membership, also deals with discrimination and came into force in January 1991.

Implications of trade union membership.

Broadly speaking, it is interpreted as being discriminatory if an applicant is refused, or obstructed from obtaining, a job because of trade union membership. Paradoxically, it is also now no longer necessary for a candidate to belong to a trade union to get a job.

Where an applicant feels they have been discriminated against in the above situations they have the right to appeal to an industrial tribunal. Where the case is decided in an applicant's favour the employer concerned will be penalised; part of the compensation may be given as an award for injury to the applicant's feelings.

Contracts of employment

Verbal offers of employment.

Managers should be aware of current legislation and how it affects a job offer. As soon as a verbal offer is made and accepted, a contract of employment is made. An example of this is where a person is offered a job by telephone, subsequent to being interviewed a few days earlier. The contract is legally binding and an attempt to rescind the offer would be a breach of contract.

Written offers of employment.

Job offers should therefore only be made in writing where any conditions of employment can be defined at the same time; for example, 'subject to satisfactory references' or 'subject to a satisfactory medical examination'.

Definition of full-time staff.

All new employees recruited to work more than 16 hours a week are classed as full-time staff and as such must be given a written contract of employment within 13 weeks of accepting the post. This is defined in the Employment Protection (Consolidation) Act 1978 and must set out the main terms and conditions of employment and benefits. More information on this matter and a sample form are given in Chapter 4: Preparing for recruitment.

Employment Agencies Act (1973)

Agencies must be licensed.

This Act was introduced to regulate employment agency operations. It requires all agencies to register with the Department of Employment from which they are licensed annually, and also makes them liable to inspection. If you are obliged to use an agency you should ensure that the firm is currently licensed to conduct this type of operation.

Fees.

The Act lays down certain rules on when fees may be charged for candidates. Agencies are not permitted to charge persons registering with them for work, whether they are placed or not. The exceptions are theatrical performers, fashion and photographic models.

Overseas workers

Work permits.

All persons subject to immigration control must have a work permit before starting employment in the UK. (This does not apply to EC residents.)

Certain conditions must be met; it is not simply a case of an aspiring applicant writing in or making a personal call to get work. Among other stipulations, the prospective employers must show that they are unable to fill the post locally or nationally. The onus is on the employer to make an application on form OW1, obtainable from a Job Centre or employment office.

Employers must prove they cannot recruit within the UK.

The formalities are formidable and can be lengthy. Unless there is some special reason for taking on someone from abroad, it is advisable to avoid anything but local or national recruitment.

Legislation on health matters

Health and Safety at Work Act.

The Health and Safety at Work Act (1974) lays down legislation that makes employers responsible for the health, safety and welfare of all staff.

Medical screening.

A medical examination, required by many firms for new employees, is optional and not a legal requirement. An exception is the case where it is known the new employee will be working in a hazardous or dangerous environment such as diving operations, certain chemical plants and other areas where toxic substances are being worked with.

Jobs where health screening is recommended.

A guidance note entitled 'Pre-Employment Health Screening' has been issued by the Government Health and Safety Executive. This is obtainable from HM Stationery Office and recommends that medical screening should take place whenever a new employee is engaged to:

- undertake work considered hazardous to workers unless certain medical criteria are met by those doing it;

- work where there is a danger in the transmission of disease;
- do work requiring high levels of physical fitness; for example, handling heavy weights;
- work in an environment which is new to them; for example, where they will be exposed to varying levels of heat, cold or air pressure.

Many of the above are already covered by statutory regulations where a medical examination is necessary prior to employment; for instance, drivers of HGVs and PSVs.

More information and advice for employers is available from the Employment Medical Advisory Service in their local municipality.

◀ CHAPTER 3 ▶

JOB ANALYSIS

Once it has been decided that extra staff are needed the current way of working should be investigated. Operating procedures must be monitored and individual tasks examined in detail.

Assess overall work operation.

During this process shortcomings may come to light. Your aim at this stage is to assess the overall work operation to see if things are done in the most practical and economical way. This applies to all firms no matter what their function. It could be difficult in an office and may involve informal chats with key staff members. In an industrial area it may be easier to ascertain the function and work practices of a department or section. But in all cases it will mean visiting the place of work operations, observing what is going on and, if necessary, discussing the matter with line supervisors.

When this has been done, there will be two options:

- recruit additional staff in the same capacity as existing workers;
- recruit staff to perform new tasks that have come to light as a result of the work investigation.

Internal promotion.

Promotion from within is always to be recommended when a new post is envisaged. It shows that management recognise the work of individual members of staff and are prepared to reward effort. From the management's point of view there is less doubt about the postholder fitting in than there would be with recruitment from outside – provided the right selection is made. Recruitment is then confined to replacing the lower-grade vacancy that would arise.

Job evaluation

A job evaluation programme is set up to determine:

- the job that requires to be done with associated tasks;
- the ideal person to undertake the tasks.

All jobs in a firm should be evaluated at some time. This means the periodic monitoring of existing work functions, to take into account new tasks that may have been introduced since the last evaluation.

Task of job evaluation.

Job evaluation involves noting all the contributing factors of a job of work. It takes into account the skills and attributes of the staff member needed to perform the tasks and the environment in which the duties are undertaken. It is similar to the initial work observance mentioned above but will have to be in much more detail. Whereas the original exercise was to see how the work could be improved overall, this project covers just what is being done by individual members of the workforce.

Job description

Job descriptions give a summary of the tasks, skills and responsibilities of a job. They can only be realistic if you analyse the results of an overall job evaluation exercise. This is conducted by a firm either for its entire workforce or for single jobs that are to be reassessed. In this way the job description of all posts can be amended when the tasks of a job change.

As manager, you will already have a good idea of the tasks of the job to be evaluated but you now have to know everything about the job. This will mean a discussion with the local line supervisor, a visit to the place of work and probably a chat with the person performing the job function.

Questionnaire

Getting workers to fill in a questionnaire on job tasks.

If the work is not obvious it is useful to get a member of the staff undertaking the job to fill in the questionnaire. An example is given on page 33. This is a sensitive area and the person completing the questionnaire must be assured that it is not a time and motion exercise; his/her output is not being measured and the quality of work is not being questioned. It should be explained that there is simply a need to record the actual tasks being performed in all jobs.

Workers asked to complete a questionnaire may be inclined to over-

Job description questionnaire

Job title Department	Responsible to Responsible for (No of persons)

Give main purpose of job

What knowledge, skills or qualifications are required?

Describe main tasks

List any supervisory or managerial responsibilities

List other responsibilities - money, equipment, materials.

Please use other side of sheet to give further details on any item

Compiled by .... Date ....

Examples of job description format

JOB TITLE	Name by which job is usually known
DEPARTMENT	Section of firm where postholder will be working
REPORTS TO	Job title of person the postholder is responsible to
LOCATION	Only necessary when it is expected that the postholder will be employed away from the main office. Also used when extensive travelling or periods away from main office will be required.
PURPOSE OF JOB	Outline of the scope or function of the job.
MAIN TASKS	Summary of the main duties
TASKS	Describe the job in not more than ten separate sentences. List and number them in order of importance. Sentences should be short; tasks are best described in action verbs using the present tense. Keep this style throughout the list. Be specific as far as possible. As an example, the tasks of an assistant in an advertising agency would appear as: • types proposals, press releases and features • collates and files press information • liaises with the media by telephone • keeps diary of appointments for account managers
EXPERIENCE OR KNOWLEDGE REQUIRED	For the above position this section would be used to specify keyboard proficiency, word-processing experience and other office skills. It could also indicate desirable and essential educational or technical qualifications
OTHER RELEVANT REQUIREMENTS	This section is used to specify any other factors of the job. It could describe the working environment, conditions and any constraints. It could also list any attributes or characteristics of the ideal person for the job when a person specification is not available.

emphasise their duties and, where tasks are of an intricate nature, the supervisor should be called on to verify the content. It is quite in order for a number of workers undertaking the same task to be asked to contribute to this exercise. Some will enter items that others may be inclined to miss or consider insignificant, so a more realistic picture of the tasks of the job will result.

Although not referred to on the questionnaire, it can be useful to record the most difficult tasks as well as any unpleasant aspects of the job. Details would be obtained during the job evaluation and only recorded if they were significant. They could be entered under a heading of 'Other Relevant Requirements' on the job description form proper, shown on page 34. A note of this will be handy when drawing up a job specification, and, more importantly, when making your final selection. It could help you to avoid making a disastrous choice and employing someone with attributes that indicate they would be totally unsuitable.

Limitations of questionnaire.

The reliability of a questionnaire on its own is entirely dependent upon the literacy of the completer and his/her appreciation of what is required. Therefore, in many cases it may be necessary to have an informal interview with the postholder actually performing the tasks. The greater the input at this stage the more authentic will be the final job description.

Writing the job description

Job descriptions must be complete and take into account all aspects of the work performed.

Using the completed questionnaire together with information and notes taken during discussions, your task is now to draw up a job description which will describe the purpose of the work, the duties and responsibilities of the postholder, the scope of the job and who the postholder reports to.

Invite comments on final draft from workers.

In its final form the job description may consist of one or more pages depending on the complexity of the job. It should be written in a standard format with the same section headings being used for all job titles to allow comparisons with any other job as necessary.

An example of the layout and content of a job description is given on page 34.

Although effectively a management tool, there is nothing secretive about a job description or a person specification. In fact, it is essential that when the former is in draft form it should be shown to the postholders it portrays with the idea of confirming the content. Some important factor could well have been lost during transcription. To be of use, a job description must be factually correct and the only true way to ensure this is to discuss its content with a person performing the job.

Uses of job description

The job description can be useful in many spheres in the personnel area. Two important uses are for evaluating different jobs in a grading exercise and as background information for pay negotiations. It can also contribute to training and manpower scheduling. During recruitment it can be used for:

- drawing up a person specification (see pages 39 and 46);
- a reference aid when writing staff vacancy adverts;
- part of an information pack to send to prospective employees;
- a ready reference for an interviewer or panel member during the selection of candidates.

Aid to BS5750 certification.

The writing-up of job descriptions for each job in the firm is also a first step for companies working towards BS5750: Quality systems certification. One requirement of a quality management system is that each staff member should be aware of his/her responsibilities and of what they are expected to do in the course of their work. These facts are confirmed during a job evaluation exercise and recorded in the job description of each postholder.

Job descriptions should be regularly updated.

When completed, the job description is filed and remains as a permanent reference to a particular job. It should be updated at least every 12 months and more frequently when there is a known change in the scope or content of the job.

Examples of job descriptions

The descriptions shown on pages 37 and 38 are useful as a guide to the format used. Some comments are given on how they were written.

Secretarial support

The description of a member of the secretarial support to an account manager in an advertising agency is given on page 37. This is easily contained on one A4 sheet. A separate person specification for this post was not considered necessary as the requirements are fairly general. They are thus condensed and included in the final paragraph of the

Price Advertising: job description

JOB TITLE	Secretarial Support
DEPARTMENT	Technical Services
REPORTS TO	Technical Services Manager
RESPONSIBLE FOR	Nil
MAIN DUTIES	Provide secretarial support to Technical Services Manager and other account managers
TASKS	1 Types: • contact reports • press releases • miscellaneous letters and text 2 Compiles and updates mailing lists 3 Keeps diary appointments for Technical Services Manager and account managers 4 Identifies, cuts, collates and files press cuttings 5 Produces, collates and packs press releases for collection by carrier or Post Office 5 Maintains and updates magazine and journal racks 6 Provides back-up for reception and telephone in event of absences 7 Operates computer terminal on iocal area network.
OTHER RESPONSIBILITIES	Contacts computer support firms with fault details when necessary
KNOWLEDGE OR QUALIFICATIONS	Secretarial skills including: • touch typing at 30wpm • WP experience - WORDPERFECT preferred • experience of working in a small, busy office

Price Advertising: job description

JOB TITLE	Receptionist
DEPARTMENT	Office Services
REPORTS TO	Administration Director
RESPONSIBLE FOR	Nil
MAIN DUTIES	Provide initial company contact for telephone, mail and personal callers
TASKS	1 Greets all callers to the office 2 Handles initial enquiries on all matters 3 Receives all incoming telephone calls and: • routes them to required extensions • takes messages for absent staff • routes and books overseas telephone calls 4 Opens all incoming mail and distributes to addressees 5 Types outgoing and delivers incoming faxes 6 Keeps register and allocates the use of conference and board rooms for meetings 7 Makes travel arrangements for staff 8 Keeps track of whereabouts of staff 9 Orders couriers, taxis and makes other transport arrangements 10 When required, assists with post franking and other office functions.
CIRCUMSTANCES	Working for busy marketing company of some 70 employees.

description. This is a procedure that can often be adopted for jobs where no special attributes are identified.

Receptionist

Monitoring revealed true workload.

The job description of the receptionist on page 38 is the result of an actual job evaluation. It is contained on a single A4 sheet.

The true description of the post was only determined after observation and consultation with the person holding the job. It is fairly obvious after reading the description that the expression receptionist is something of an understatement. From the duties listed it can be seen that the position is virtually a Man (or Girl!) Friday.

At the start, the receptionist filled in a questionnaire but underestimated her contribution to the firm. She recorded only the basic jobs that a person in this position would normally perform. After checking by an independent observer, the tasks of dealing with faxes, making travel arrangements and other duties came to light. The company was extremely fortunate in the incumbent; it was apparent that extra responsibilities had been gathered over a period with her agreement and the complete picture of her tasks was only ascertained after a friendly chat. She was a person who enjoyed being busy and active.

It is essential that the full extent of these duties is noted and recorded. Should she ever have to be replaced, the firm would expect the same effort from her replacement. But under the basic job title of receptionist, the true state of affairs would not be evident to an applicant and the replacement might be shocked by the work he/she was expected to handle. This is a prime example of how useful a job description can be. Unless all the tasks of a job are fully documented and made clear during the recruiting process, misunderstandings and problems are inevitable.

Senior project engineer

The job description of a senior project engineer is shown on page 40.

As this was a new post, many of the tasks were academic. The originator had probably drawn on similar tasks of other engineering posts for most of the information; this is acceptable and the only course of action in the circumstances.

In cases like this, a job evaluation exercise should be conducted within a year. This will reveal the anomalies of the original description and enable a more authentic document to be used in the future.

Person specification

The person specification is a written schedule of the desirable character-

Baker Engineering: job description

JOB TITLE	Senior Project Engineer
DEPARTMENT	Overseas Engineering
REPORTS TO	Overseas Engineering Manager
RESPONSIBLE FOR	Three project engineers, five technicians plus local labour
LOCATION	At any designated overseas site
PURPOSE	Control of operations on construction site
MAIN DUTIES	Responsibility for fabrication work and technical expertise on defined section of large engineering project
TASKS	1 Plans and supervises construction work on engineering installation 2 Co-ordinates activities of the project team with the work of other disciplines of the company 3 Liaises with management and senior engineers of other companies engaged on installation 4 Interprets engineering drawings and specifications 5 Decides on field modifications as necessary 6 Manages all company staff on site 7 Controls finance and budget for local expenses 8 Hires and manages local labour 9 Submits regular progress reports to management
OTHER INFORMATION	Position is at overseas location. Remote with limited hygiene and social facilities available.

istics and qualities of a person to fill a particular job vacancy. The job description is used as the main source of information but the writer will have to add other items; for example, where the holder of a post has contact with the public. In these circumstances, temperament and diplomacy are just as important as any specialist knowledge. The various tasks are evaluated and a mental picture is devised of the type of person who will best be able to do the job. The completed person specification is then used as a yardstick by which the attributes of applicants seeking to fill the job are compared.

When drawing up a person specification the key duties of the job should first be grouped together in a particular area: physical requirements (if any); technical knowledge; the need to liaise with others, etc. These should then be translated into the appropriate skills needed to do the job.

Seven-Point Plan

Person's attributes under key headings.

To guide compilers of person specifications, a number of plans have been devised over the years. One of the foremost is the Seven-Point Plan.

This provides seven key headings which denote the make-up of a person. These seven points are expanded with notes describing the attributes that the person best suited to handle the job should have. The seven elements are:

PHYSICAL CHARACTERISTICS	Any special demands of the job - for example - lifting. Alternatively, the desirability of a good speaking voice for a telephonist and smart appearance for a receptionist.
ATTAINMENTS	These are broken down into qualifications, the skills needed to do the job and experience in the particular type of work.
INTELLIGENCE	This describes the mental level, reasoning power and ability to analyse.
SPECIAL APTITUDES	For example, communication skills.
INTERESTS	The type of interests that could best be used in the job. Alternatively, what leisure activities appear to be compatible with the job.

DISPOSITION	For example, personality, dependability, motivation.
CIRCUMSTANCES	The special conditions that apply to the job. For instance, the need to work away from home occasionally or be part of a team on shift work. Another point worth mentioning would be that the work is done out of doors.

When drawing up a person specification you must be objective in your approach. One danger is to visualise the qualities of the previous holder of the post and use them as a basis. This could lead you away at a tangent and land you in all sorts of difficulties. The job description and your observation of the work must be your only source of information.

Be specific when describing tasks.

Always be specific and precise when writing a person specification. 'Ability to communicate' and 'numerate' are too vague. It is much better to use 'able to give clear technical instructions capable of being easily understood by recipient' and 'able to add, subtract, multiply and divide to two decimal places - able to produce percentages from supplied figures'. Clerical ability could be translated as 'able to sort, file and retrieve letters, memos and reports'. There will then be no doubt as to the tasks of the post and the ideal person required to undertake them.

Level of expertise required.

When it can be determined, identify the level of expertise required in a certain area. 'At least three years' experience in a small sales office' is preferable to 'good general office experience'.

Physical attributes.

Don't forget the physical attributes required of the job holder if they are relevant. This will apply to heavy manual work and working in areas subject to extreme hot or cold conditions.

State actual qualification requirements.

Where necessary, specific qualifications should be indicated for GCSEs, O and A levels. For CSEs, the minimum grade desirable should be stated to give an interested job applicant some idea of the standard required.

Educational requirements are often combined to show the holder's overall ability but there will be occasions where individual subjects should be stated; for example, where the job consists of tasks involving academic subjects - laboratory assistant (chemistry) and compiling statistics (mathematics or statistics). Any acceptable alternative qualifications should be listed.

Remember that this is a record of the *total* criteria an ideal person employed to do the job should be capable of. You are not restricted in wordage; at this stage you must be sure that *all* the information is set down to serve as a comprehensive source of information on the type of person required. When eventually you need to write a press advertisement you can extract the most significant facts.

Ensure full details are recorded.

Main factors of a person specification

Here is a summary of the main factors to consider when drawing up a person specification.

- What experience, training or qualifications are necessary to do the work?
- What physical attributes are relevant? Must the postholder be exceptionally strong (to lift weights) or of at least average height to reach items associated with the job?
- Is the job routine or is initiative required? How difficult is the job?
- What responsibilities are involved? Does the postholder control staff, cash or materials?
- What amount of supervision is required?
- What is the job environment? Is the work performed indoors or outdoors? Is it isolated? Does it result in little contact with other workers?
- What special attributes are required for the job?

Do not over-estimate the individual attributes required. Also, beware of being too specific and narrowing the requirements down to standards which may be difficult to meet. It is a good idea to state two grades of either qualifications or experience - desirable (or preferred) and essential. This could result in ten years' experience being desirable with a minimum of five years being essential. For a technical engineering post it would be desirable for applicants to have a degree and preference would be given to graduates. However, following this with a statement about an essential requirement of an HND or HNC broadens the range. Admittedly, it will increase the response from a job advertisement but it could mean not having to re-advertise, which you might have to do if no engineer with a degree applies for the job.

Clarify what is desirable and/or essential.

A more informal way of expressing this requirement when drawing up an advertisement is to say, 'The ideal candidate will be . . . . and have . . . .'

A person specification will be shorter than a job description and

Price Advertising: person specification

JOB TITLE Receptionist
DEPARTMENT Office Services

	Essential	Desirable
EXPERIENCE AND QUALIFICATIONS	Two years' operation of small PBX telephone system Knowledge of telex operation	Good knowledge of overseas telephone and telex circuits
	Knowledge of routine of busy office	Keyboard proficient at 30wpm Work in a similar capacity in a firm of some 70 employees
	O level English language (or GCSE equivalent)	Three O levels (or GCSE equivalent) and secretarial skills
PHYSICAL CHARACTERISTICS	Smart and well dressed Clear speech and good telephone manner	
DISPOSITION	Pleasant personality, cheerful and friendly Reliable	Alert and active Able and willing to work under pressure at times
APTITUDE	Communication skills Able to relate to other staff members at all levels	Self motivated Able to make decisions and use initiative
GENERAL INTELLIGENCE	Alert mind and above average intelligence	Quick to grasp information

Baker Engineering: person specification

JOB TITLE Senior Project Engineer
DEPARTMENT Overseas Engineering

	Essential	Desirable
EXPERIENCE	Has had senior responsibility for a small project or acted as project engineer on a large or medium sized project, preferably in the petro-chemical or a related industry Overseas experience on engineering complex	Has directed, controlled and co-ordinated a small engineering project overseas. Has managed the activities of assigned project personnel in the planning, scheduling, design quality and execution of the project. Alternatively, has functioned as a senior project engineer on a large or medium-sized project Has experience in supervising both UK and foreign nationals to ensure standards are maintained and schedules met
QUALIFICATIONS	Degree or HND/HNC in engineering	Chartered engineer of a relevant institution, or equivalent
PHYSICAL CHARACTERISTICS	Physically fit	
DISPOSITION	Must be a good mixer	
APTITUDE	Communication and man management skills	Motivated, self reliant leader able to get the best out of subsidiary staff

should generally be contained on one A4 sheet. But, as with the job description, the format should be standardised and used for all types of job, irrespective of length. The same headings may not be used for every type of job but, when they are, they should be in the same sequence as on the form and thus be easily identifiable and capable of comparison.

Examples of person specifications

The layout may follow any design but it is useful to set the essential and desirable requirements of any elements in columns. In this way they are easily identified and compared.

Receptionist
A person specification was essential to set down the special characteristics of this particular position. See page 44.

Senior project engineer
As this was a new position no definite information was available. Previously there had been one engineer handling the job but expansion required more staff and it was decided to appoint a section head for the project.

As in the preparation of all person specifications, the majority of the requirements were assessed after studying the new job description. These, together with data gathered from similar posts, were combined to give a fairly good description of what is expected of the future postholder. See page 45.

◀ CHAPTER 4 ▶

PREPARING FOR RECRUITMENT

In this chapter we cover preliminaries that must be considered and preparations to be made before the recruitment programme can begin. In the main they consist of making sure that the required forms are available. You may already have some in use but wish to compare them with the layouts suggested in this chapter and check whether it would be worthwhile updating them.

Have the forms ready before recruitment begins.

It is particularly important to have all the forms ready *before* the recruitment programme starts. Running out in the middle of the project and having to await the printer's pleasure could seriously hamper the campaign.

You must decide how you wish prospective applicants to make their initial approach. You will therefore end the job advertisement with the expression, 'Send CV', 'Write or telephone for an application form' or simply 'Write and tell us why you feel you're qualified for this job. . . .' Each method has its merits and limitations.

Response by letter

Applications by letter.

This method can save time, work and expense by thinning out the number of totally unsuitable applicants who will inevitably apply for the post. The more enthusiastic job seekers will send in a letter and attach their CV anyway. However, asking for a letter will save the bother of sending out application forms to those writing in who are obviously not worth considering. You should be able to tell by the format and content of a letter whether or not the prospect is worth considering. Asking for a letter is often preferred for more senior positions. Suitable candidates will relish the idea of promoting themselves and setting down their attributes, whereas unsuitable and unqualified applicants may well feel unable to attempt this and thereby appreciate that the job is not for them.

Use of curriculum vitae

Using CVs to deal with applicants.

Requesting a CV is a speedy way of handling applications. Unnecessary postal exchanges are eliminated; a CV can be checked and a promising candidate identified and called to interview in the time it takes to respond to a request for an application form.

Apart from the content, the presentation of a CV generally says something about the applicant. Have time and thought gone into the layout or is it simply a list of jobs held in reverse order? A professionally produced CV can generally be detected and you must decide why the originator decided to use this service, and whether it is relevant to the job application. Was the applicant unable to produce it him/herself or didn't he/she have the time (or inclination)? Perhaps he/she didn't have the facilities to produce a presentable document. Again, plus points should be awarded if the applicant apparently realised his/her limitations but was astute enough to take the trouble and pay to have the CV produced. Whether or not the CV was professionally written should only be an influencing factor if the vacant post calls for the ability to produce something similar to a CV.

Use of CV gives advantage to applicant.

The CV is geared to promote its compiler in the best possible light - or it should be! The literate originator can put forward his/her better points and try to hide questionable areas. The writer is able to expand on favourite subjects, unhindered by such soul-searching questions as: 'What do you consider your main achievements?' or the even more poignant, 'What are your strengths and weaknesses?' This is obviously to the applicant's advantage and to your disadvantage unless you are shrewd enough to realise gaps, omissions or errors exist in the presentation. However, the purpose of a CV is to obtain an interview and its content can (and should) be verified during any subsequent meeting.

A poorly structured, rambling CV is often a nuisance and may influence you against someone who may otherwise be an ideal candidate for the job on offer. A well-compiled CV is easy to read and should display the important points of the applicant sufficiently well for them to be quickly recognised. If it portrays a person who has taken the trouble to spend some time on the presentation, although the content may lack certain prerequisites for the job, you may well feel it is worthwhile interviewing the originator.

The CV is also useful for the job seeker intent on making random approaches for work. Any CVs querying unsolicited job vacancies should be acknowledged and filed for future consideration.

Use of application form

One limitation of the CV, no matter how well presented, is its non-compatibility. It is unlikely that two presentations will be similar and thus 'qualifications' on one may be prominently displayed while on another may be hidden away. This is no great inconvenience if you have only a few to scrutinise but lists of relevant items may need to be drawn up if there are many applications to evaluate.

Advantages to employer of using application forms.

The order of layout is the one great advantage of the company application form. Each applicant's credentials will be in the same place. And you will (or should) have designed your application form so that the most important attributes in a candidate are readily located.

Points to look for in completed application form.

There are other advantages of using an application form from the company's point of view, apart from the opportunity to ask searching questions. It can often reveal certain characteristics of the job applicant even before the content has been studied. The applicant is expected to complete it in his/her own handwriting and this often reveals important features. Was the form hurriedly completed, with sentences squeezed in as an afterthought, or did the applicant make a trial run on a photocopy and so produce a well-written document? Were there smudges, creases and coffee stains on parts of the form? Were all the questions answered or was 'not known' or 'not applicable' written in the spaces opposite difficult questions? Worse still, were these spaces simply left blank? Handwriting may not necessarily be a yardstick by which to judge an applicant's suitability for a particular job these days, but if it is appallingly bad the applicant should be aware of this and have therefore printed key words and expressions in capitals.

The application form may benefit some job seekers who are doubtful about producing their own CV. They may feel that they have little to promote. In these circumstances an application form can be helpful in asking specific questions and prompting relevant answers. It can thus help those not highly literate or used to working with words.

Application form versus CV.

The company may feel that its application form is essential because it contains relevant questions. But the truth is that these are invariably stereotyped and often self-restricting in their objective unless a section headed: 'Have you anything further you wish to tell us about your suitability for the job?' is included. The CV, on the other hand, can encompass significant points relevant to the job on offer. It is to the applicant's advantage to present a CV if he/she wants to promote him/herself. And this action subsequently benefits the employer by helping to narrow down the people to be called to interview.

In general, there is no reason why both methods of supplying application information should not be used. The CV can serve as the initial contact with an application form being sent out to the most promising job searchers.

It is recommended that the company application form should be completed by all candidates at some stage of the recruiting process. It will generally contain an honesty clause whereby the writer signs that everything entered on the form is true to the best of the candidate's knowledge. In theory this should eliminate any dubious claims that are occasionally made in CVs. For the candidate who is successful it will serve as background information on the personal file, and the forms of those who are rejected could usefully be filed as a database for future consideration.

Application form format

A properly designed application form is a powerful management tool. Unfortunately, many firms ignore this and fail to use perhaps the most important aid in any pre-selection process. Forms that are poorly laid out and ask pointless questions generally do nothing to enhance the company's image.

Is your application form as good as it might be?

An application form is much more useful to the employing company than a CV as it can ask pertinent questions of the applicant that a CV may conveniently avoid. Apart from providing initial information to allow the pre-selection of candidates for interview it serves as background information throughout the recruiting procedure, up to the final selection stage. Where a CV is subjective, an application form is objective and allows (or should allow) quick comparison between a specific attribute of all applicants.

An application form should not be compared to an application for, say, a driving licence. After personal details have been entered it should make the applicant think. But this does not mean that it need be difficult to complete. Where required, notes and guidelines should be given to ensure that the applicant is clear about what he/she is required to enter.

Use different forms for different vacancies.

The form need not be restricted to one type. Indeed three types of form could be used: a single A4 sheet for the school or college leaver, a slightly longer version for the general range of jobs and a further, more detailed document for executive and senior management positions. There is no restriction on length. The latter type could well use four A4 sheets. While it is not feasible for an application form to be devised for each different type of job, there is no reason why a supplementary sheet should not accompany the main form and be used for specialised posts. It could query aspects relevant to a particular job and thus the complete document could approach the CV in its subjectiveness.

One failing on many forms is the inadequate space allowed for answers. The applicant should not have to squeeze even a simple answer into one line. In all questions the amount of space allowed should indicate the size of the answer expected.

The company name and logo, if any, should be clearly printed on the form. This provides a commendable image of the employing organisation, especially if it heads a well-designed application form.

In general, questions should be open-ended which will probably mean that they will be answered in different ways by candidates for different posts. Information is sought on past experience and attainments, not hypothetical aspirations. Questions asked should therefore be realistic and factual.

Application form questions

Questions to be asked.

The following list gives some notes on questions that should be asked on every application form.

JOB APPLIED FOR	This should be in a prime position, preferably at the top of the form. To you, as employer, it is a reference and the most important piece of information.
SOURCE OF JOB INFORMATION	By analysing this entry information from the forms of successful (and other shortlisted) candidates, you can get an indication of where to advertise future jobs.

NAME	Surname/family name and first names should be requested - not just initials.
ADDRESS	It must be made clear that the address given is where the applicant can be contacted.
AVAILABILITY FOR INTERVIEW	This is useful as it saves time and effort when drawing up a shortlist.
GUIDELINES	These should be given so that the applicant fully understands what is required.
EXPERIENCE	It should be made clear whether this means job-related experience or simply skills held.
INTERESTS	On its own this is limiting. It is better to remove doubt by using the heading INTERESTS, HOBBIES AND LEISURE ACTIVITIES. Ask how much time the activities take up each week.
REFERENCES	As well as the names and addresses, ask for telephone numbers.
QUALIFICATIONS	Use a layout that will extract all the information. This will discourage the use of, say, HNC by a person who does not hold this certificate.
STATUS OF HEALTH	Only a short statement is needed. More information can be obtained on a medical questionnaire nearer to the end of the recruitment programme. This question can usually be combined with a query about disability.

What not to include on the form

There is no need for such self-assessment queries as: 'What are your future aspirations?' and 'What are your main strengths and weaknesses?' Even 'Why are you applying for this post?' is inane, especially when the form is being completed by a person who has been out of work for the previous two years!

There is no set answer to these questions and they do not contribute to the recruitment programme. They may have been inserted on the recommendation of a psychologist, but unless this specialist is on hand to interpret the answers they will mean little to the average recruiter. If these questions are to be asked they should be kept for the interview.

Avoid discriminatory questions.

Do not ask the applicants for their marital status or the number of their children. These questions could be construed as an attempt to discriminate; for example, when a woman is applying for a position that necessitates shift working. If the information is subsequently required for personal records or for employee life insurance cover it should be requested in a separate letter which clearly states the reason.

Examples of application form

The examples on pages 54–57 cover all types of recruitment.

Example A is page 1 of an all-purpose form and may be used for college leaver, graduate, general or semi-skilled worker, and executive/ management applicants.

Example B is the second (and final) page of an application form for college leavers and the average workforce.

Examples C and D serve as pages 2 and 3 of a form suitable for management and executive applicants. This form concentrates on obtaining details of the current or most recent position and also provides space for brief notes on previous jobs. It enables basic facts to be set down without going into too much detail on topics that could more easily be covered in an interview.

In all cases there is the opportunity for applicants to give details about special experience or other relevant facts that they feel make them suitable for the job.

Conditions of employment

Contract of employment.

It is a statutory requirement that all employees classed as full-time staff must be given a written contract of employment, setting out the main terms and conditions of their engagement.

It should record the following minimum terms:

- names of the parties
- job title
- date employment started
- length of notice required to and from an employer

Continues on page 58.

Example A: application form

ABC COMMUNICATIONS LTD

Post applied for

PERSONAL DETAILS

Surname/family name	Date of birth
	Nationality
First names	Tel no (work)
	Tel no (home)
Address where contactable	

When are you available for interview?	When could you start?	How did you come to hear of the vacancy?

SECONDARY EDUCATION

Schools attended	Dates from - to		Subjects studied (include failures)	Grade or pass level obtained

HIGHER EDUCATION

Place of study	Dates from - to		Qualification	Result

MEMBERSHIP OF PROFESSIONAL INSTITUTE OR BODIES

Name of body	Date elected	How obtained	Grade of membership

Example B: application form

ABC COMMUNICATIONS LTD APPLICATION FOR EMPLOYMENT

EMPLOYMENT RECORD

Name and address of previous employer	Job title
	Employed from to

List main duties and responsibilities

Reason for leaving	Salary on leaving

Name and address of previous employers	Position held	Dates from - to

OTHER INFORMATION

Is there any illness or injury that might affect your current or future work capability? YES/NO (If yes give details)

Are you registered disabled? YES/NO If yes give RDN

What are your main interests and activities outside work? *How many hours per week do you spend on each?*

Give details of experience or other information relevant to your application for this post

I declare that the information given above is correct to the best of my knowledge. I will undergo a medical examination if required.

Signed .... Date ....

Example C: application form

ABC COMMUNICATIONS LTD APPLICATION FOR EMPLOYMENT

EMPLOYMENT RECORD

Name and address of current/last employer	Nature of business
Job title	Employed from to
Show with diagram how you fit into the organisation	Salary on joining £ Current/latest salary £
	Give job titles of people reporting directly to you
	Were you promoted during time with this firm?
List main responsibilities and duties	
What were your reasons for leaving?	

Name and address of previous employer	Job title
	Employed from to
List main duties and responsibilities	
Reason for leaving	Salary on leaving

Example D: application form

ABC COMMUNICATIONS LTD APPLICATION FOR EMPLOYMENT

EMPLOYMENT RECORD continued

Name and address of previous employers	Position held	Dates from - to

OTHER INFORMATION

Is there any illness or injury that might affect your current or future work capability? YES/NO (If yes give details)

Are you registered disabled? YES/NO If yes give RDN

What are your main interests and activities outside work? *How many hours per week do you spend on each?*

Give details of experience or other information relevant to your application for this post

Give the name, address and telephone number of two references who know your work

I declare that the information given above is correct to the best of my knowledge. I will undergo a medical examination if required

Signed .... Date ....

- normal hours of work
- rate of pay, how calculated and the method of payment
- length of holidays and holiday pay arrangements
- pension arrangements and, in particular, whether or not the employee is 'contracted out' for NI purposes
- procedure for grievances and the company rules about any disciplinary action
- the employee's right to belong to a trade union.

The make-up of the agreement will depend on the job and the employing organisation. In some cases the terms and conditions may be set out on a single A4 sheet of paper and presented in the form of a letter. The new recruit will sign and return a copy, retaining the original. In larger firms a special booklet may be produced defining certain aspects of the conditions of engagement. The booklet or other separate information is referred to in an accompanying letter and the applicant is asked to sign and return an acknowledgement slip. An example of a suitable form is given on page 59.

The following notes expand on some of the terms used above:

JOB TITLE	As well as the job title it is useful if the company job description for the post is given to the new applicant, if not already supplied prior to the interview.
PAY	In addition to the rate and payment date the pay scale should also be given. Where applicable, reference to travel loans, cheap mortgages, luncheon vouchers, private health insurance and other fringe benefits should be recorded here.
HOURS	The hours per week should be specified together with the normal daily attendance times. Reference should also be made to the working of shifts, flexitime and other possibly unsocial hours.
OVERTIME	Where this is to be worked, details of whether it is voluntary or compulsory should be recorded together with the

Conditions of employment

Name of employer Date employment commenced	Name of employee Job title
PAY	£ per annum Day of payment
HOURS OF WORK	Hours of work per week Daily working hours
OVERTIME	Voluntary/compulsory Overtime rate per hour
HOLIDAYS	Amount of holidays Rate of holiday pay
SICKNESS	Sickness and sick pay Company sick pay (if any)
PENSION	Contracted out YES/NO Contributory/non-contributory
NOTICE	Due to employee Due to employer
DISCIPLINARY RULES AND GRIEVANCE PROCEDURE	
Employee's signature	Date

	payment terms; either time off in lieu or payment at an hourly rate.
HOLIDAYS	The number of public holidays should be set down together with holiday pay arrangements. Annual factory shut-down dates should be recorded if applicable.
SICKNESS	Terms and conditions relating to illness and injury should be recorded, including qualifying periods. Statutory sick pay as well as any company pay schemes should also be recorded.
PENSIONS	It is obligatory to state whether company employment is contracted in or out of the state pension scheme.
NOTICE	There are statutory periods of notice: a minimum of one week from an employee after a month's service; the same applies from an employer for employees with up to two years' service and one week for each year after that up to a maximum of 12 weeks. Where the employer wants to extend these periods it should be recorded here.
DISCIPLINARY AND GRIEVANCE PROCEDURE	The grievance procedure must be outlined and indicate the person to whom the complaint should be made and whether in writing or verbally. Disciplinary rules, procedures, penalties and appeals should be recorded or referred to in another document where they are laid down.
UNION MEMBERSHIP	This section may be added where applicable.
REFERENCES	This section can be added to record the title of any reference documents that form part of the terms of employment but are too long or detailed to cover on this sheet. For example, pension rights and conditions and a company employee handbook.

Recruitment Code

The Institute of Personnel Management has published a Code of Recruitment which is a standard for the profession. It encourages and explains the best practice for all types of recruitment.

IPM.

The Code covers recruitment procedures and all aspects of recruiting including advertising, selection technique, interviews and the process of obtaining references. There is also a section on using external recruitment organisations such as agencies and consultants.

Code explains all recruitment procedures.

Copies of the Code are available from the IPM at IPM House, Camp Road, London SW19 4UX. You should enclose a stamped addressed envelope.

Another booklet on the subject is published by the Advisory and Conciliation Arbitration Service (ACAS): 'Advisory Booklet Number 6: Recruitment and Selection'. It can be obtained from regional offices of ACAS (address from local Job Centre) or from ACAS head office at 27 Wilton Street, London SW1X 7AZ; 071-210 3000.

ACAS.

Record of recruitment

It is essential to maintain some record of the recruitment programme. It can be as simple or as complicated as you wish but it should serve as an ongoing check and as a historical record of the operation. The layout of a suitable form is given on page 62. The actual advertisement should be photocopied and attached to, or kept with, the form. A new form will be required for each job advertisement.

Record the results of each advertisement.

The form gives details of the job and the type of advertisement used and in which publication it appeared.

There is a sequential number in the first column to show the total ongoing applications. In the second column the applicants' names should be entered in block capitals.

In the third column an abbreviation is used before the date to denote the type of initial approach; that is, LET for letter, CV for curriculum vitae and TEL for telephone query. Under 'Sent' will be AFM for application form, ACK for acknowledgement or REJ where the application is to be rejected as not worthy of further consideration.

Abbreviations are used after the shortlisting evaluation to decide who is to be invited to attend for an interview. Here INV will be used followed by the date the letter is sent and the actual interview date. Unsuitable applicants will again be categorised as REJ.

The final column gives the result of the assessment after the interview

Record of recruitment

Record of recruitment

Job title	No of vacancies
Date(s) advertised	
Display or classified	
Publication used	

Number of replies			
After 2 days		Replies by letter	
4 days		telephone	
6 days		using CV	
8 days		callers	
later		Total number of replies	

NO	NAME	INITIAL CONTACT				AFTER SHORTLISTING			RESULT	
		Recd	Date	Sent	Date	Sent	Date	Intvw date	Sent	Date

Use abbreviations in columns thus:

LET - letter
ACK - acknowledgement
CV - curriculum vitae
TEL - telephone
AFM - application form
REJ - rejected
INV - invitation
OFF - offer of job

has taken place. OFF indicates an offer letter while REJ again signifies an unsuccessful candidate.

Analysis of response.

A simple analysis, as at the top right-hand corner of the form, can be completed when the recruitment programme is over. The response after a given number of days will indicate the build-up of replies over the period. This can be useful in future recruitment when planning dates to be kept clear for interviews. The breakdown of replies by different methods will also help in the future to ensure that the most popular approach is adequately prepared for.

◀ CHAPTER 5 ▶

SOURCES OF STAFF

There are many ways to recruit staff but recruiters must decide which best suits their needs. The choice will depend on the type of job on offer and to what extent you, as recruiter, wish to take part in the recruitment and selection process.

Summary of staff sources.

New staff can be found from the following sources.

- press advertising
- recruitment consultants
- executive search
- recruitment agencies
- Job Centres
- schools and colleges
- internal recruitment
- unsolicited applications, held on file
- previous unsuccessful applicants, held on file.

The list is not in any particular order; the first source to be consulted could well be the list of previously unsuccessful applicants!

Press advertising

In this medium are included the national dailies, regional and local newspapers, free newspapers, magazines and trade journals.

National dailies

National press for specialist, technical and management positions.

Advertising in the national dailies will only be realistic for specialist, technical and management positions and where you know that you need national coverage.

The cost is high in the quality press. Currently, £86 per single column centimetre in the *Daily Telegraph* means thousands of pounds for a multi-column display but provides a circulation of 1.1 million and insertion in the *Sunday Telegraph*. Charges are marginally less in the tabloids. In the national editions of the *Daily Mirror* the cost is £83 for the same space but with a circulation to over 3 million readers. In all the national newspapers, certain job disciplines are advertised on specified days of the week.

The advantage of this medium is speed. Advertising can usually be placed within a few days with the paper of your choice, and directed at the appropriate socio-economic group you consider will include the type of person you want to recruit.

In all but the classified advertisements of the above newspapers you will encounter design and artwork charges as an extra. If you seriously feel that this is the outlet for you and you intend to use this medium frequently, it is wise to seek the advice of an advertising agency.

Regional and local press

Regional or local newspapers where there is local expertise.

The regional and local press can be useful for advertising certain technical and middle-management vacancies. You will obviously not be considering distant applications, but will feel that there should be sufficient expertise locally. This type of publication obviously has a much lower circulation but one that could prove adequate for your requirement. Moreover, the cost will be much less.

Local newspapers generally appear weekly and carry a limited amount of display advertisements. One advantage is that they are often read over the weekend and their exposure per edition is greater than for the national dailies which are discarded daily. Senior or executive positions are rarely seen in these newspapers.

Free newspapers

Freesheets for jobs up to supervisor level, when you need to fill a vacancy quickly.

This is a medium that appears to be growing. The free newspapers are very localised and, probably because of this, a considerable amount of space is given to advertising, some comparable to national display standard. They rarely cover jobs above technician or supervisor level. Being locally oriented, there is a growing practice of simply including a telephone number, thereby indicating a preference for a quick transaction. An interview can be arranged over the telephone and a suitable applicant may be engaged in a few days.

This type of publication often has columns for part-time and temporary work which could serve as a good source of staff to the smaller firm wanting workers for a short period.

Magazines and trade journals

Best for specialist staff but forward planning needed.

The disadvantage of this type of publication is that it generally appears monthly (or even quarterly) and this, together with the length of time required to prepare and place the advertisement, makes the overall process a lengthy business. You will therefore have to plan ahead. Readers know of this limitation and often view job advertisements in this type of publication with a certain amount of scepticism.

If you are using other sources of recruitment in addition, you will probably have to delay pre-selection to take into account the response from journals.

On the merit side there is the specialisation factor of the trade or professional journal. You are directing your requirement to people who you know will be interested in or at least have some knowledge of whatever theme the magazine covers.

Advertising the job

Preparing the advertisement. Size and style depend on the post.

The time spent in drawing up and the subsequent cost of publishing the advertisement will depend on the type and level of the job to be offered. For a senior position it is almost as important to promote the company image as it is to describe the job function, and a double column display will provide ample space to do this. For a junior or general post in the organisation a few lines in the classified section may be sufficient.

You can determine the advertising costs of the publication suggested from BRAD: *British Rate and Data* gives information on all British national and local publications. A copy is generally available in the reference section of most public libraries.

Writing the advertisement

Any advertisement must satisfy the following requirements:

- It must reach the right group of readers.
- It must attract their attention.

- It must describe the position realistically.
- It must promote the correct company image.

Reach the right people.

To reach the right group of people the first task will be to select the advertising medium which will be read by that group. In the event of this being a newspaper, care will be needed in the wording of the title so that only the right people will be attracted. Advertisements in trade journals can dwell more on the functions of the job. In both cases, your prospect will need to be attracted and encouraged to read what you have to say. The headline should be designed to do this. It should be clear - not catchy or ambiguous.

Deter unsuitable applicants.

As well as attracting the right people it is useful simultaneously to deter unsuitable people. You must therefore be concise, factual and describe the functions of the position realistically. Do not be vague and romanticise the job or try to be clever, conveying little or nothing about the post. Otherwise, you will invite a large response from a wide audience, and you will find yourself with extra work during pre-selection.

Salary and benefits.

State the salary to be paid clearly. Don't use the word 'negotiable'. This can promote a bad image of a firm keen to get the best from offering the least. If you are uncertain of the salary (which you shouldn't be), don't mention it at all. Depending on the space available, mention benefits. If the vacant post is at senior technical or middle-management level, don't be afraid to ask for essential qualifications or experience; this is another method of discriminating against the wrong type of person.

Use a logo to promote the company's image.

Take the opportunity to promote the company even if only by displaying the name in heavy type. A lot of people reading the advertisement will have no intention of applying for the job, but this is no reason why they should not be given a good impression of the firm. A logo will enhance the image.

Avoid disciminatory text in the advertisement.

Be careful you do not inadvertently use discriminatory sentences in any part of the advertisement. The text should be worded so that there is no doubt that the job applies to people of all racial backgrounds and both sexes.

Tell the reader clearly how to apply.

Make it clear how the interested applicant should apply for the job and whether he/she should send a CV. Give a personal name in the address to contact; this puts each application on a personal level and encourages the applicant to feel he/she is communicating with a person and not a title. Spell out the address clearly and include the post code. If you are geared up to accept telephone enquiries, give the number and the name to ask for. (And make sure the person named is aware of, and prepared for, the calls.)

Don't use a box number for job advertisement.

Never use a box number. It will severely reduce the response which could mean losing some of the most promising applicants. It implies that the advertiser has something to hide!

Examples of advertisements

There are plenty of examples of job advertisements in the daily press and you will be able to use the best layout for your requirement by studying them.

The first example on page 69 shows how *not* to write a job advertisement. It is vague and tells the reader nothing about the work or the employing company. We assume that it is in a technical environment as the postholder will assist the works manager, but again the position may be completely office bound. Most people see themselves as conscientious so this is no criterion. It states that applicants should be experienced, but in what? Typing, computers, shop floor operation? People who feel they could be interested are unable to telephone for more details as only written replies are asked for via a box number. This advertisement will invariably attract a large response. The advertiser will have to spend time sorting through CVs and letters until he/she is able even to start thinking about a shortlist. Perhaps the compiler is unsure just what is wanted!

The second example, shown on the same page, will attract applicants with a suitable background. Experience and qualifications are listed so there is no doubt about what the candidates should have. Next, a list of tasks is given and although brief they are sufficient to enable an interested job searcher to form a picture of what the job is about. Only a progressive company would offer training on CAD systems.

Placing the advertisement

You should contact the selected press medium before starting to write the advertisement content. They have the expertise and will be able to advise on the form the advertisement should take and any discounts available for insertions on a number of successive days.

Discuss your requirements with the publisher's advertising department.

You will be able to discuss the best size, position and date for the insertion. They will be able to suggest borders to give your text an added impact.

They will offer to prepare artwork but there will be a charge for this. If you have the use of a desk top publishing system in your firm you could

Personal Assistant

Due to expansion we have a requirement for an assistant to the works manager.

Persons applying should be experienced or keen to learn. Conscientiousness and an eye for detail are necessary.

A good salary is offered with 20 days per year holiday. Holiday arrangements honoured.

Write for application form.

Box 88, Northern Advertiser, Nottingham.

How not to write an advertisement

Technical Drawing Assistant

A minimum of 12 months' drawing office experience is required for this position in a busy plastic fabrication company. Preference will be given to applicants with ONC.

Tasks include:
- producing engineering drawings from artists' sketches
- amending and updating existing drawings
- maintaining computer database of engineering records

Facilities to obtain CAD/CAM experience.

Write or phone for application form to: Elaine Peterson, PROCOL DESIGN, Woodburn Estate, Willesden NW4
Tel: 071-376 3926

A good advertisement which will attract suitable applicants provide camera-ready copy. Once you know the constraints of the size of the advertisement, you will be able to experiment with sizes of type and produce a professional display.

You should keep a record of all job advertising, in addition to other records of the recruitment campaign. It is then easy to refer back to specific styles and displays that you used on certain dates and the response they produced. A cutting of the actual advertisement as it appeared is the best record. Stapled to an A4 sheet, the dates and other information can be written below it.

Recruitment consultants

Services offered by consultants and what they will cost.

Recruitment consultants are specialised, high-profile organisations. They will take over virtually all your recruitment chores. They will design and draw up advertisements, place them in suitable publications and handle the recruitment selection down to a shortlist of between 6 and 15 suitable candidates - a major campaign, in fact.

Their charge is usually based on a percentage (normally 20 per cent) of the first year's salary of the person finally selected. Advertising and interview expenses are extra. These types of organisation often employ consultants who are technically qualified and experienced in the discipline of the job tendered for. Psychometric and other types of testing may be used by them on candidates.

This type of consultant may also conduct variations of the above. They may handle the advertising, evaluate the CVs or application forms and send you a batch that they think you will be interested in. In both these situations the name of your firm as the recruiter is not revealed until the shortlist stage.

Advantages of using a consultant.

An advantage from your point of view is that the service is swift - shortlists are usually ready three weeks from an advertisement appearing. And with a reputable firm you are assured the vetting from a technical and character-appraising viewpoint has been accomplished. You will, of course, interview the prospect but you are able to concentrate on the compatibility factor; whether this eminently suitable applicant will fit into your little empire.

Executive search

There is a special type of consultant who concentrates on tracking down and recruiting very high calibre executives and high-flyers. They are often known as headhunters.

Headhunting the high-flyers.

One in five senior positions were filled by this method according to a survey conducted in 1990 but the ratio is greater for executives in the £50,000+ salary range. There are ten large companies operating in this field and the number is growing. Many have databases holding the names and locations of thousands of possible candidates and often exchange and 'deal' in them with others in the same line of business.

Methods of the headhunters.

From a submitted brief, executive search specialists begin an operation of careful evaluation and search for a suitable specialist currently employed in competitive firms in the same line of business as their client. The initial approach is by telephone, when the person being hunted is asked if he/she would be interested in another position. This is the start of a programme of often clandestine meetings in which the consultant confirms the suitability of the fortunate individual. The name of the predatory firm is not divulged until the final stages.

If you feel the person to fill your vacant post can only be recruited using this method it will cost you around 30 per cent of the first year's salary, plus interview expenses. The search can be world-wide if required.

Initially, the headhunter will need a job description, person specification, salary range and list of benefits, and thereafter will maintain a close liaison with a client. Most firms offer a further search if the hunted leaves within six months.

There are two associations of search consultants: the Association of Search and Selection Consultants and the Executive Recruitment Association. Advice and other information on suitable search consultants can be obtained from the Management Consultant Advisory Service, 38 Blenheim Avenue, Ilford IG2 6JQ.

The question of ethics inevitably surfaces in this method of recruitment, although there appears to be a gentleman's agreement that headhunters will not poach from their clients. However, firms considering this service are often reticent, considering that they themselves could be made vulnerable. Merely entering into discussions with an executive search operator could, they feel, provide an opportunity for any visiting consultant to learn something of their own company. Their reasoning is that the identity of their own high-flyers could be ascertained, and they in turn made susceptible to an approach by the headhunter at a later date.

Recruitment agencies

Employment agencies have a pool of labour on their files.

Employment agencies cover the lower end of the recruitment market. Their number has more than doubled in the last ten years but this growth has now levelled off, owing in part to government licensing and inspection.

Agencies advertise in the press and often use a high street position to display the jobs on their books. They work a little in advance of recruitment consultants. Whereas the latter usually take a brief and set out on a recruiting sortie, agencies have a permanent pool of labour on file, waiting for employers' requirements. Their scope ranges from the short-term hiring out of temporary workers to the filling of permanent vacancies.

Recruitment agencies are obviously keen to place anyone in a job as they work on commission. And this is perhaps one of the shortcomings of using this type of recruiter. They are inclined to put aside the person specification that the employer may have supplied (or widen the scope to suit themselves) and often send unsuitable applicants after jobs. This may in part be because of the standard of the recruiting staff in the smaller agencies. In some cases it seems they push as many applicants forward as possible in the hope that at least a percentage will be successful. This can be particularly frustrating to an employer who may not have had time to read the CV sent ahead and be into the interview before realising that the applicant is not up to the standard expected.

Using an agency is much less expensive than a recruitment specialist, rightly so as they deal at the lower end of the market. Many agencies specialise in a particular type of work, such as accounting or secretarial posts; a few handle only technical positions.

If you do use an agency you are advised to ascertain and agree the terms in the first instance. And even if you are asked to complete one of their application forms, always send the job description and person specification for the post you want to fill. This will avoid any misunderstanding. It is better to use the services of an agency that has been recommended by a satisfied user.

Job Centres offer a free service and are particularly useful for semi-skilled and technician grade vacancies.

Job Centres

Job Centres are an often under-valued source of labour for the small business. Although they rarely handle vacancies above middle management, they can provide a good range of semi-skilled and technician grade jobs. This is particularly so in big towns and areas where there is a surplus of large firms using certain specialised types of labour.

A Job Centre is especially useful to a small growing business as the service is free. But you must make it work for you. There have been isolated reports of apathy among the staff which appear to have been passed on to job seekers with the result that many feel that it is a waste of time registering there. If you have a requirement you should ask to speak to the local manager and explain your needs. Establishing a rapport with him/her will ensure that your needs are clearly understood. This is a government agency; you have a right to expect an acceptable level of commitment and service and the Job Centre has an obligation to provide it.

You will not get the vetting of applicants that an agency would provide so you will have to be prepared to do your own pre-selection and interviewing. But Job Centre staff often telephone with details of the person they think may be suitable and you can discuss certain points before seeing the applicant.

School and college leavers

If you need to fill junior or apprentice vacancies, plan ahead.

There will be fewer school leavers in the coming years. Owing to a declining birthrate from the early 1970s there will be a marked drop in students leaving school or college from 1991 - almost a 25 per cent fall from the 1988 level. There will also be virtually no growth in graduate output to cope with the envisaged high demand in the high technology sector. It could therefore be difficult for the small employer to fill junior or apprentice vacancies by the more usual methods of press advertising.

If you need to employ school or college leavers it is essential that you work out a campaign for junior recruitment now. It should concentrate on the personal approach.

For a start you should make yourself known to the Careers Advisory Officer of the school most likely to supply your needs. Confining this to an occasional telephone call is not enough. Pay him/her a visit and offer to speak to students who are due to leave in the current year about your company and its products. You could also invite the Careers Officer to your premises. You could even set aside an afternoon a month so that groups of sixth formers can be shown round the firm. Make yourself known to the headteacher and also to teachers of subjects relevant to your operation.

Another idea is to sponsor some part of the school or college activities.

This need not be expensive; for example, a donation of some of your services or products to the school, if this is feasible. You could also pass on a personal computer after upgrading. It is important to promote your company name in the minds of all attending the school as a firm that it would probably be nice to work for.

Internal recruitment

In-house transfer or promotion is more efficient than recruiting cold from outside the organisation.

Filling a vacancy from within the company either by promotion or lateral transfer is convenient and cost-effective. Even if further training is needed it is a more efficient method than starting to recruit cold from outside the organisation.

There are a few ways of achieving this:

- good ongoing communication between departmental managers and supervisors;
- an internal memo from a section head to other departments announcing an expected vacancy;
- a regular spot in the firm's newsletter or news-sheet
- a section of the main internal notice board and any other departmental display areas.

As mentioned earlier, careful appraisal of the internal workforce is also the recommended path for promotion as well as the means of averting a dismissal owing to redundancy.

Unsolicited applications on file

Keep your file of unsolicited applications, as well as runners up for past vacancies.

There are a number of job seekers who make direct approaches to firms where they think there may be vacancies. Occasionally they use the telephone but usually a CV and a letter of enquiry will be sent.

This is a valuable source of future labour. All enquiries should be filed, preferably in some sort of category of work, and checked through at the start of any recruiting programme. The benefits are obvious. If a single vacancy can be filled from the waiting file it will eliminate:

Achievable savings.

- the advertising costs (or the expense of using an agency or other recruitment specialist);
- the administrative costs of drawing up a shortlist;

- much of your own time in the early stages of preparing a recruiting campaign.

All applications received that you feel could meet your needs in the future should be noted and acknowledged. (A sample of a suitable letter is given below.) When a vacancy occurs it may be worthwhile using the pre-screening telephone procedure to assess suitability. If the

Ref:

Date

Miss Elaine Johnston
Rose Cottage
Franklins Moor
Princes Risborough
Buckinghamshire
Post code

Dear Miss Johnston

STAFF VACANCY

Thank you for submitting your curriculum vitae.

Unfortunately we do not have a position for which we feel you would be suited at this time. However, we should like to keep your information on file and will contact you should a vacancy arise in the near future.

Thank you for the interest you have shown in the company.

Yours sincerely
for PREST & COMPANY LIMITED

Clive Prendegast
General Manager

applicant seems promising he/she could be offered an interview before a large-scale programme is started. Even if his/her suitability meets only the essential requirements, there is every reason to include him/her in the interview programme. There is one thing in this person's favour: he/she had the initiative and interest in your company to make a speculative approach in the first place.

Other sources

Local radio

Local radio is occasionally used as a means of recruiting secretarial staff and certain engineering posts at technician level. However, the listener audience at any one time is not readily determinable. It may be usable for part-time workers where a run of daily announcements is made but its value for specific, one-off jobs is questionable.

National TV

The Oracle and Prestel services of national TV stations are beginning to gear up for recruitment, albeit in a limited way. At the moment the chief users appear to be agencies in search of computer programmers. However, it is reasonable to suppose that this method could be extended to display marketing and financial executive positions in the future.

Notice boards on the perimeter wall attract the attention of passers-by.

External notice boards

This is a cheap way of attracting local labour for a variety of trade and semi-skilled positions. Even if the firm is not on a main thoroughfare, a prominent board will be seen by some passing traffic and observers will be keen to pass on this information to friends and acquaintances who are out of a job. Where this method is used, telephone and reception staff should be told and instructed how to respond to callers on the telephone and in person. In both cases, applicants should be given an application form and told who in the firm to address them to.

Ex-service organisations

Some Ex-service associations maintain lists of members who are actively seeking work. The range of expertise can cover any of the innumerable trades in use in the three main services, the Royal Marines and, to a lesser extent the police force. If there is no suitable person at the time of contact it may be worthwhile leaving details of any vacancy on file with the relevant re-employment officer.

Recommendations from existing employees

This is a means of recruitment that presents itself occasionally. A current member of the workforce notes the details of a vacant job from a newsletter or an internal notice board and says he has a friend who is ideal for the job. If the person is a trusted employee and a good worker there is reason to believe the friend will be too.

However, there is a negative side to this arrangement that could be counter-productive, especially if the vacancy is in the person's own section.

The usual selection routine should be applied to employees' recommendations.

The fact that the person was recommended should not mean any change in the selection routine and the proposed candidate should undergo the same processing as others who have applied for the job. There should be no easy entry after a brief informal interview. The main concern is that a clique in a particular section or department will be established. This could easily happen if a key member introduces a number of applicants for a successive string of vacancies. The establishment of a close group could well get out of hand and be objected to by other members of the workforce. The question of discrimination could also arise if the friend is of the same ethnic group and sex. In a one-off situation this form of introduction can work well but any repeat of these circumstances should make the recruiter aware of the dangers.

The older employee

Taking on people over 50 could result in a more reliable and dedicated workforce.

There is a wealth of labour in the over-50 age group and even in pensioners. Owing to the higher standard of living in recent years, the older generation is experiencing better health, and with improved medical knowledge people are staying fitter and able to work much longer.

The average age of the working population has increased steadily over the last 25 years – not everyone retires at 65! Depending on the type of work, the over-50s can make a worthwhile contribution to any workforce. Employees will also probably have a higher standard of time-keeping, conscientiousness and overall ability to do the job. And in certain types of work their experience will probably be unequalled.

The Association of Retired Persons has recently set up an organisation to help place older people in jobs. Operating in conjunction with a major employment agency, Age Works aims to provide a nation-wide service to all older job seekers. Details are available from Age Works, Bedford House, 3rd floor, 69–79 Fulham High Street, London SW6 3JW; 071-371 5411.

◀ CHAPTER 6 ▶

PRE-SELECTION OF CANDIDATES

Once the advertisement has appeared you have a short respite. The anticipated rush of enquiries requesting an application form can be dealt with by secretarial staff but the record of recruitment sheet should be completed on a daily basis. You should also make arrangements for any telephone enquiries to be directed to a member of staff who is able to deal with them.

Acknowledging applications

Send letter with application form telling applicant who to return form to.

If you asked applicants to write or telephone for an application form, a letter should be sent with the blank form indicating who the completed form should be sent to. An example is given on page 79.

Where you have asked for a CV you could also send the applicant an application form. However, if the applicant looks promising and an interview seems likely, you could leave this formality until the meeting. It depends on the type of information you have on hand to compare with other candidates. In either case the receipt of the CV should be acknowledged as soon as possible, if only to avoid telephone calls asking if you have received it. An example of this type of letter is given on page 80.

Avoid telephone queries by acknowledging all applications.

Acknowledge all applications. This is the professional approach and it saves the nuisance of applicants telephoning to enquire about their suitability. The acknowledgement should be non-committal and simply state that the application is being considered. Applicants will obtain

Ref:

Date

Mr Eliott James
Garbitts End
Nether Franklington
Near Peterborough
Northants
Post code

Dear Mr James

VACANCY – STOREKEEPER

Thank you for your application for the above position.

Please complete the enclosed application form and return it to the undersigned as soon as possible.

Yours sincerely
for WESTLAND MOTORS LIMITED

P C Ryder
Stores Manager

some satisfaction from the fact that their application is not being dismissed out of hand.

Unsuitable applicants

Early vetting of applicants is advisable.

It will be possible to vet some applicants from their first letter or certainly their CV. Where application forms have been sent out indiscriminately it will usually be obvious from a glance at the returned forms that some applicants will be non-starters – where you know that sitting on the application form for a week is unlikely to change your decision.

Ref:

Date

Mrs E Crowther
166 Northern Road
Northallerton
North Yorkshire
Post code

Dear Mrs Crowther

VACANCY – WP OPERATOR

Thank you for your CV and application for the above position.

We will shortly be evaluating applications and will write to you on this matter in the near future.

Yours sincerely
for ARGOSY PUBLICITY SERVICES

Gillian Frobisher
Office Manager

Write to unsuitable applicants as soon as possible.

In these circumstances it is courteous to let them know that their application has been unsuccessful straight away. Many people apply for more than one job at a time and, when the result of one application is known, job-hunting energies are channelled in a new direction. An example of a letter for this purpose is shown on page 81.

You can never afford to be specific about the reason for rejection. If you give a reason, there may be repercussions in the form of a telephone call attempting to challenge your decision. There is some encouragement in letting the candidate know that his/her application and credentials will be held on file but only if you intend to do this, of course.

Ref:

Date

Mr J B Mortimer
14 Queens Road
Leicester
Post code

Dear Mr Mortimer

VACANCY – SENIOR ACCOUNTS CLERK

Thank you for your recent application for the above position.

After carefully considering your application I am sorry to have to tell you that we have decided not to ask you to attend for an interview on this occasion.

I hope you will be successful in finding another suitable position.

Yours sincerely
for ACME TRADING COMPANY LIMITED

Philip Brown
Divisional Manager

Evaluating the response

After responding to requests for application forms you are ready to evaluate the recruitment exercise to date. The first factor to consider is the degree of response and, by this, the effectiveness of the advertising.

Problems of too many replies.

If there have been a large number of replies with a high proportion of unsuitable applicants you will need to check your advertisement and the medium used. It has obviously been too vague and thereby attracted too wide a response. This will mean more work for you in checking each approach made and inevitably the chore of sending off rejection letters to those obviously below the standard required.

Perhaps your wording about the requirements was not sufficiently clear. Did you specify the essential qualifications or experience required? Admittedly, in times of high unemployment, there will be replies from many aspiring applicants who are below standard but who will try to convince themselves that they stand a chance of an interview. This is a further reason for spending some time on the advertisement and ensuring that it is directed only at the group of people who you feel will best be able to fill the vacancy.

It is necessary to keep clear records of the advertising used and the degree of response in order to compare the results with other campaigns (see page 61).

Pre-selection techniques

Methods to assess quality of applicant.

You must now decide what yardstick to use to determine who will be called for interview. The number of replies received should not influence this decision. You are not interested in vetting a set proportion of the applicants. You are primarily concerned with the quality of the applicants, especially those whose attributes meet a certain threshold or minimum standard.

The completed company application form together with the person specification will help you here. An impressive CV will have aroused interest but this medium is difficult to use when comparing applicants. It is hard on the eyes as well as the brain as comparable attributes will not be presented uniformly. This is perhaps one of the chief advantages of the application form in the selection process.

For a start you must decide what parameters to use. Initially these will be from any of the following:

- experience
- qualifications
- X factor.

Before making any assessments you should spend a few moments reading the application form as a report. Can you determine why the writer has applied for the job? Is he/she unemployed now? What sort of previous jobs were held? Is the work record complete? Are the answers to the questions embroidered unnecessarily? What is the handwriting like? If outrageously poor or indecipherable in places, could this affect any tasks of the vacant job? Some of these items may fall into the X range (explained below).

Look for experience supported by qualifications.

Experience is undoubtedly the most important attribute and, provided it is supported by the appropriate skills, it will be the first yardstick in the selection process. In the person specification the desirable and essential levels of experience, skills and qualifications of the ideal candidate will be identified. Initially, you will be checking credentials against the desirable elements in the person specification but you may have to lower them later.

Using the X factor.

The X factor is simply your personal feeling on what other features you think the ideal candidate should possess, based on the information before you and your personal knowledge of the job. It could be the structure of a CV, an impeccably compiled application form or even the person's leisure-time activities. While not contributing directly to the selection process they may influence you and provide a pointer that makes you feel the person would be worth seeing. When you get this gut feeling, you should act on it.

The shortlist.

You should be considering a final shortlist of around six for a single post - more, of course, if there are several positions to be filled. However, at this stage your aim is to eliminate the bottom half of the applicants and you should be able to do this using the above constraints.

You may be able to draw up your shortlist from the above factors but it is likely you will need to use other attributes to influence your choice. Remember, you are not always seeking merit points. Detrimental features that warn you that a person would not fit into a particular job are also important. Some points to check on the plus side are:

Using positive and negative points.

- a notable achievement or success during past employment
- promotion during previous employment
- the type and depth of leisure activities
- a school record - grades of GCSEs/CSEs and A levels attained.

Negative points which are important:

- an unusual number of jobs held in a given period
- glaring omissions which may be accidental (carelessness) or deliberate
- a significant point which convinces you that the applicant will be unsuitable.

It is more important to see all suitable candidates, and to ensure that a good prospect does not slip through the net, than to be too restrictive in the numbers called to interview.

Using the person specification.

You must keep to your original plan of only considering those applicants with the essential qualities listed on the person specification. The X factor and other deliberations should only be used on applicants who meet this requirement. If this level is not attained by any applicant it will mean re-advertising the position. Before this you must check that your outlet was suitable and that the advertisement was worded to attract the type of person wanted. Perhaps the salary quoted was too low and the benefits package inadequate? Going further back, it may be worth looking seriously at the person specification and job description and considering if your thoughts on the grading of this threshold were perhaps unrealistic.

Points system

If you have difficulty in deciding which prospective candidates are worth interviewing from the basic details you could consider using a points system with, if necessary, a weighting formula. This procedure can also be used to arrive at your final choice.

It involves giving a number (say between 1 to 10) when assessing the main attributes of an applicant. For example, qualifications, experience, achievements, leisure activities and computer knowledge could be marked as 8, 6, 2, 5 and 4 points respectively. This indicates that the applicant earns 25 points out of a possible 50. But although mathematically correct this may not give a realistic picture. Among the different elements you are assessing you may feel that some are more important than others. The main one will usually be experience but not always. It may be that the person sought also needs to be highly computer literate. In this case, the points allocated to this category could be weighted by a multiplying factor of 2. The above individual's final points total would then be 29, which might be enough to put him/her ahead of rivals who may have had one or two additional points allocated to them for experience. This can often provide a useful pointer as to who, within a group of equally promising applicants, should be selected for an interview.

Use of weighting system for most important attribute.

Qualifications

Qualification equivalents.

It is useful to recognise any qualifications that candidates indicate on their CV and application form.

The Business and Technician Education Council (BTEC) awards in England and Wales and the equivalent Scottish Vocational Education Council (SCOTVET) certificates in Scotland are called National Diplomas and Certificates, like their predecessor, the OND/HND and ONC/HNC.

Diplomas in general are awarded after successful attendance of a period of full-time study, certificates after part-time (evening or day-release) study.

Although the syllabus depth of OND is greater than ONC, both are of comparable standard. ONC and OND approach GCE A level in comparable subjects.

Higher National Diplomas (HND) approach degree standard. HNC is roughly the same standard as HND but covers a narrower range of subjects.

It is remarkable how infrequently qualifications are asked for at interview. Some applicants bring them to the meeting and offer them for examination. But in a few cases when I have asked for sight of the qualifications claimed to be held, I have been met with a blank stare. The excuse has usually been that they didn't think they would be asked for.

Insist on seeing proof of qualifications.

Proof of qualifications should always be asked for. In some suspect cases I have written to the applicants requesting a photocopy. But in half of these there was no response and, of the rest, half stated that they had failed the final qualifying part of the examination. Their application was not considered further. It is apparent that the listing of qualifications on a CV cannot always be taken as representing the true state of affairs and, if there is any doubt, proof must be obtained. In the suggested layout for an application form shown on page 54 we offer a means of reducing dubious claims on the qualifications held by candidates.

It is not feasible to give a list of even the more common professional qualifications here. A comprehensive guide to educational, technical, professional and academic qualifications is contained in the current edition of *British Qualifications*, published by Kogan Page.

Telephone screening

This method of screening is useful in any pre-selection process. It can

Record of pre-selection telephone call

NAME OF APPLICANT [ ]

Enter details before starting call.

Is that [ ]

My name is [ ] and I'm phoning about your application for a job with [ ]

I wonder if you'd care to clarify a few things about that application?

I see you are currently employed by [ ]

Information obtained from CV or application form.

Why do you want to change?

or

What have you been doing while unemployed?

What specially made you apply for our position? Do you know much about our company?

Have you any questions you want to ask me?

	Poor	Average	Good
Speaking voice	☐	☐	☐
Use of vocabulary	☐	☐	☐
Standard of questions asked	☐	☐	☐
Enthusiasm noted	☐	☐	☐

Disposition Friendly ☐ Non-committal ☐ Guarded ☐

Other observations:

Signature of caller .... Date ....

eliminate the non-starters and, associated with other factors, help you to decide whether it is worth asking an applicant to attend for an interview. It is best used on borderline cases where some of the details in the CV or application form (the X factor?) make it appear that the applicant is not up to standard but where you have a gut feeling that he/she may be worth seeing.

Eliminate unsuitable applicants.

The procedure involves asking questions from a checklist similar to that shown on page 86.

Ideally, the call should be made to the home but if this proves fruitless and the applicant seems promising he/she should be telephoned at work if a number has been given. Remember to ask if the applicant is free to talk. He/she may share an office. If necessary, offer to call back.

The first part of the form is completed before you make the call. Whether or not the applicant is in employment can be ascertained from the CV or application form. A line should then be drawn through whichever state does not apply to ensure that this question is not accidentally asked. You should also have the person's application form or CV handy.

The actual questions are not really important, but they need to be sufficiently probing to provide some response from the person - and that is all you need. You are trying to form a picture in your mind of the speaker at the other end of the telephone. You have to try to imagine just what sort of a person he/she is.

Be friendly and patient in your opening; your distant applicant must be given time to collect him/herself.

Enter the replies in the space below the questions. You will be able to judge the person's spontaneity after inviting them to ask questions. They may be reticent about doing this but encourage them to make conversation - another topic may present itself.

If the telephoned applicant is forthcoming you could delve a little deeper and discuss his/her experience or suitability for the post, referring to the application form as necessary.

The call need only take about 10-15 minutes. Once you feel you have an idea of the person's make-up you can end by saying you will be in touch. You make no commitment to an interview at this time.

Is the applicant worth interviewing?

The rest of the form should now be completed. You should have spent sufficient time talking to assess whether it is worth proceeding with the application. Judgement on the speaking voice will not be so important where tasks in the applicant's job does not include talking to the public either in person or by telephone.

Evaluate the conversation.

There may be occasions where the person called appears reticent and shy about discussing himself at all. He may seem to be over-cautious and guarded when answering your questions. Again, this should be considered only in the light of the future position. It is obviously not the trait of an energetic salesperson but this characteristic is not necessarily a minus point for a person in, say, a technical position who will be working for long periods on their own. Also, this technique is fairly new and the recipient of the telephone call may well be taken completely by surprise (and may even think it is someone playing a practical joke).

After evaluating the call and entering your comments on the form you must decide whether to invite the person for interview. This exercise is only a preliminary in the process of recruitment but it can eliminate immediately totally unsuitable people and also give credence to interviewing an applicant who, on the strength of his application form or CV, did not appear to be worth seeing.

Second assessor

Always use second assessor.

It is essential to have a second assessor of the job applicant as to rely entirely on your own judgment is a precarious path to follow. With the best of intentions you could be guilty of being subjective without realising it.

The contribution of the second assessor may be as light or as concentrated as the situation demands. It could mean a brief chat with someone who will be working in the same area or a full scale interview using the same format as yourself. Wherever possible it is advisable that this should be a technical assessment and conducted by a supervisor who has control of the tasks of the vacant post. It could include any one of a variety of tests that have been devised to assess the post.

All opinions should be recorded.

The results should be documented; an opinion expressed during a brief chat is not good enough. Even if the meeting is confined to a few questions, the second interviewer should be prepared to write a short report on the person interviewed and if possible offer his/her recommendation on whether or not the candidate should be offered the post.

Planning the interview

Pick times that will not clash with other commitments.

With the shortlist drawn up you are now ready to plan the interview.

Dates and times should be set that will not interfere with other commitments and not have to be cancelled. For senior and important technical positions it is useful to allow two hours per interview. This allows one and a half hours for the interview and a further 30 minutes for writing up notes. The personal meeting could well last only an hour, but this will be a bonus and enable you to be ahead and so avoid having to keep candidates waiting beyond their appointment time. You should not consider seeing more than six candidates in a working day.

Allow $1\frac{1}{2}$ hours per applicant.

You must consider how the interview will be conducted. Will you be the sole interviewer? Wherever possible it is recommended that at least one other interviewer should be used at some stage, even in the smallest firm, as a second opinion is always useful. This could be a technical assessment by a line or departmental manager. Again, it may be realistic to have a group or panel interview with up to three assessors meeting the candidate at the same time. In these circumstances it is essential that all the panel members have a copy of the job description in advance and also a copy of the candidate's application form. The disadvantage of this type of interview is making sure that all the panel are available at the same time.

Plan how interview will be handled.

The ideal scenario is an initial personnel or management interview with the candidate, followed by a relatively informal meeting with the head of the department where the successful candidate will be working. These one-to-one interviews generally prove to be the most beneficial. You, as the first assessor, would probably take the candidate to the intended place of work, introduce them to the section head and stay a few minutes until the applicant regains his/her composure. The section head would then continue the interview in his/her own way and form a second opinion on the suitability of the candidate.

If your office is unsuitable you should make arrangements for other office accommodation to be available on the day. It should be comfortable and quiet. It need not have a desk; the applicant may be more at ease if the environment is made as informal as possible.

Choose a quiet area for the interview.

You will need to decide if any tests are necessary. As well as psychometric tests, there are trade or technically related tests which are best sanctioned and organised by the section or department head. There are many psychometric test programmes available but we do not intend to expand on them here, except to stress that any such test must be valid and reliable. Any dubious tests could seriously affect a candidate's performance and question your company's image.

Consider what tests may be used.

A letter must be sent to the selected candidates in good time with the request that the appointment be confirmed by letter (if time permits) or telephone. During the scheduling of interviews, consideration should be

Send letter in good time.

given to candidates with some distance to travel by arranging their appointment in the early afternoon. Clear instructions on the time and place should be given together with an estimate as to how long the

Ref:

Date

Ms Eileen Richardson
362 Boundary Road
Norwich
Post code

Dear Ms Richardson

VACANCY – EVENTS COORDINATOR

Thank you for returning our application form for the above position.

We would like to discuss your application further and invite you to attend for an interview on 14th August 1991 at 3pm.

A plan of our location is attached. You should initially report to reception and ask for Graham Walker. We anticipate you being on our premises for 1½ hours.

Please confirm you are able to attend by telephoning my secretary, Caroline Pearson, on extension 211 as soon as possible.

I look forward to meeting you on the 14th.

Yours sincerely

Graham Walker
Operations Manager

Enc. Site plan

process will last. If the candidate will be expected to undertake any form of test, this should also be mentioned.

An example of a suitable letter is given on page 90. It can often be helpful, especially to applicants who are unfamiliar with the area, to enclose a small map with suggestions about the method of travel and directions as to how to reach the site of the firm. If you intend to give a travelling allowance or provide any other expenses to the candidate you should mention it in the letter.

A job description for the post should also be sent with the letter.

Tell reception staff to expect applicant(s).

The receptionist, or the person who greets the candidates for interview, should be told of the planned interviews and given a list of expected applicants. The receptionist should be informed about any unforeseen problems so that short delays can be explained to the arrivals. In these circumstances, the offer of a coffee or a soft drink will in part compensate for the delay. A supply of company literature should be available in the waiting area. The knowledge that they are expected will go a long way to making the candidate feel at ease. It also provides the image of an efficient and caring company.

Interview day

It is useful to get in to work early to sort out any problems that may have arisen. You must take every measure possible to ensure that interviews go ahead without interruption.

Tell the people working with you that you are not to be interrupted. Make sure your telephone calls are diverted or intercepted. Make sure the receptionist has the list of expected candidates.

Papers needed during the interview.

You will need certain items to hand during the interviews:

- job description
- person specification
- applicant's CV or application form
- company literature
- an interview checklist.

Interview checklist

Recording details for assessment later.

The interview is esssentially an oral exchange between the interviewer and the candidate. However, it will be necessary to record some written comments on information elicited during the meeting. This will provide

Interview check sheet

APPLICANT ☐ JOB APPLIED FOR ☐

INTERVIEWER ☐ DATE ☐

Time check

5
5
5
5
5
5
5
5
5
5
5
5

Greeting and personal exchange. Explain interview schedule and timing.

Clarification of points on CV or application form.

Discuss relevant experience.

Main questioning from notes compiled earlier.

Describe main tasks of work and explain benefits offered by the firm.

Invite questions from candidates. Use remaining time to discuss any other relevant matter.

	YES	NO
Qualifications seen	☐	☐

+

-

Checklist of points to be covered

	1					6
Dress and appearance	☐	☐	☐	☐	☐	☐
Oral communication	☐	☐	☐	☐	☐	☐
Alertness	☐	☐	☐	☐	☐	☐
Enthusiasm	☐	☐	☐	☐	☐	☐
Composure	☐	☐	☐	☐	☐	☐

Further comments

Interviewer's signature .... Date ....

a source of data for the assessment that has to be drawn up immediately after the interview. An example is shown on page 92.

The check sheet has purposely been confined to essentials - too much writing or ticking of boxes distracts from the main issue and is offputting to the candidate. Try to make whatever notes you need while you are speaking even though this will mean looking down at the paper. This is preferable to the alternative - furiously writing comments during the candidate's answering of questions.

Plan the timing before the meeting.

The most important item is on the left-hand side of the form. This should be completed before the interview and will vary according to the applicant. The box divisions can be separated at any five-minute period, assuming the nominal interview time is one hour. Write in the subjects or important matters to be covered in the appropriate box with the time to be spent on each. Suggestions have been entered on the example. With this system you are able to keep your eye on progress during the interview and decide when it is time to move on to the next point. The main questions will be drawn up from notes you have previously made on a separate piece of paper, but if space permits you could enter some key words as reminders.

Note any plus or minus points.

The plus and minus sections are for any relevant points. They will hold brief sentences about what you feel should be considered during the interview, favouring the applicant's suitability for the post or not. Below this is a section for you to enter prompts to remind you of topics you wish to talk about during the meeting. These can be scored through as the topics are covered.

Observe an applicant's attributes and record a rating between 1 and 6.

A list of attributes that can be observed during the interview is shown in the lower section of the interview check sheet. Tick the boxes to show a rating for each characteristic between 1 and 6. Some idea of the scope of the actual rating is given below:

Dress and appearance	This will range from sloppy and very untidy to a high level of meticulousness in dress and appearance.
Oral communication	This will range from ineffective conversational ability to fluency of speech with extensive vocabulary.
Alertness	This will range from poor response and indifferent manner to acute awareness and perception.

Enthusiasm	This will range from apparent lack of interest to the showing of a keen interest in the job.
Composure	This will range from being ill at ease and tense to being relaxed and quietly self-confident.

Use key words to note characteristics.

In the remaining space alongside each subject, key words or expressions should be entered which will denote any prominent characteristics of the candidate in this area.

Some of the above may not be applicable to the job and can be ignored. For instance, alertness is an attribute that is more appropriate to a position dealing with customers or clients. For a routine job with predictable set tasks there will be no special reason for the postholder to be unduly alert.

The Further Comments section need only be completed if there is a significant factor, worthy of recording, that will help you to complete the selection rating form shown on page 112.

◀ CHAPTER 7 ▶

THE INTERVIEW

There is one school of thought that holds that the interview is a totally unreliable method of selection. This is put down to the human nature of the interviewer: he/she can never be truly objective. Any single item, no matter how small, which allows an interviewer to form an opinion of an applicant in the initial stages of the meeting can never later be wholly set on one side. It may stay at the back of the interviewer's mind throughout and thereby influence the final appraisal.

Value of interview process.

In spite of this, the interview does provide an opportunity to meet the candidate. Whether this meeting is held with any preconceived ideas or not, there has to be some value in a face-to-face session. Preparation and the way the interview is conducted can go a long way to avoid any subjectivity, however innocently it may tend to creep into the proceedings.

Objectives

You must be clear about the objectives of the interview and ensure that the conduct of it does not lead you and the interviewee on to irrelevances. The objective is to exchange information with the job applicant and in so doing obtain sufficient data to decide if the candidate:

Three attributes to be decided.

- has the experience, knowledge and qualifications to do the job on offer;

- will fit into the present working environment and get on with the staff;
- will be accepted by the existing workforce.

This is the objective from the employer's viewpoint, but it is also important to consider the job from the applicant's position. Candidates must fully understand what the work entails and be in a position to decide whether the post is the one for them.

To evaluate the above and come to a decision, the applicant must be at ease and as relaxed as possible. In fact, your initial aim will be to try to make the interviewee feel that he/she is not being interviewed at all, but simply having a friendly chat about the possibilities of a job in as comfortable an environment as possible.

Preparing for each meeting

Before each interview you must devote time to considering the candidate you are about to meet. Immediately before the meeting you should:

Tasks before the interview starts.

- review the job description and identify the main points of the person specification
- read a photocopy of the application form (or CV) and make notes on it of any unclear statements you want to query
- have completed part of your interview check sheet with the subjects to be covered.

To do this once the applicant has arrived wastes valuable interviewing time and can build up apprehension in the candidate. You will need to pick out one or two items to use as an opener to the interview proper. Make notes on a separate piece of paper.

You will have decided how long you can afford to spend on each candidate and you should use some method of timing this. (But don't take your watch off at the start and place it in a prominent position!)

Time spent on a subject will depend on job.

Allowing for an interview of at least one hour, five minutes is well spent in trying to set the visitor at ease. Thereafter the time will be spent in discussing, collecting and imparting information. How this time is divided will depend on the calibre of the job applicant. Fifteen minutes before the end of the interview period is the time to ask candidates if they have any questions. It is quite possible that something interesting will develop from this exchange and allowing too little time for discussion is a mistake. Seeming to hurry applicants' queries will give a bad impression. If there are fewer questions from the candidate than expected, the time can be usefully employed in dwelling on earlier points of the meeting that warrant expansion.

Apportion time by using interview checklist.

The interview check sheet on page 92 gives an example of how interviewing time should be spent. Depending on the job applicant, you should draw up your own schedule using five minute blocks and make a note of the items you want to cover.

It is important that the candidate appreciates that there is a structure to the interview and that the meeting is not just a session of random exchanges of views. Within the structure the content need not be followed too rigidly, provided the essential points are covered. If the candidate appears to be progressing along a slightly different route and information is forthcoming there is no need to change this. Structuring is confined to listing a few key words which remind you of points to be discussed; having them written down ensures none is omitted.

The interview will end when you hand your visitor over to the second assessor who will most likely conduct the technical appraisal.

Preconceptions about the candidate

Avoid being influenced by a previous holder of the post.

You must try to avoid having set ideas about the ideal candidate. Do not allow some item of clothing, a facial expression or other characteristic to trigger a preconceived idea. I refer to appearance, dress and manner - and do not advise you to ignore the importance of the person specification. There should be no stereotype of the right candidate and any prejudices must be set aside before the interview.

This is not always easy. Human nature, being what it is, often takes over. Negative vibes felt at the beginning of an interview may mean that more emphasis is placed on unfavourable information than on good points. Once in this mode it is difficult to reassess the interview.

Try not to make a judgement in the first few minutes.

One study on interviewing showed that a decision on whether to employ or reject (for whatever reason) is often taken within four minutes of meeting the applicant. The rest of the time, albeit unknowingly, is taken up with endorsing or, occasionally, changing this decision. Whatever decision was made initially, interviewers were inclined to concentrate on information which supported their first impression.

Be objective.

Inevitably, subjectivity creeps in and interviewers tend to endorse candidates who are like themselves. You will need a very high standard of ethics to recommend a job applicant you actively dislike! Where it is known that you will be working closely with the aspiring employee it is probably asking too much to expect this - and if this course is taken it could lead to disaster.

At the start

You should try to think yourself into an appropriately pleasant frame of mind for the interview. Try to dismiss for the time being anything about your current workload and keep your thoughts on the task ahead.

Think positively and believe that you are about to meet a good applicant for the job. However, don't let your imagination run riot or you may be in for a let-down. Where you have just completed a previous interview you must not try to compare the two candidates at this stage.

Make the candidate feel at ease.

Your first aim is to make the applicant feel at ease as quickly as possible. If this is done a more realistic interview will follow.

To reach this goal, the interview area environment must be regulated and orderly. There must be no uncertainty. And this should extend from the candidate's first approach to the receptionist to the time when your visitor is seated in a chair opposite you. There must be no reason for apprehension to build up. Thus the precautions mentioned at the end of the last chapter must be carried out (see page 91).

The person you are going to meet may be a self-assured type, doyen of many interviews and able to take everything in his/her stride. But it is more likely that the pulse will have quickened, a flush may be coming on and the interviewee will be suffering from anxiety. You have to allay this anxiety.

Wherever possible it is wise to make the effort to go to the reception area and introduce yourself. A smile and a friendly greeting are essential.

When you reach the interviewing area you should seek to relieve your visitor of any accoutrements. Coats, handbags and briefcases are best left in an outer office. This avoids the situation where the job applicant enters the area unaware of what to do with his/her briefcase/handbag etc.

If it is a panel interview and other interviewers are present, introduce them to your guest slowly, so that there is time for their names and positions to be assimilated.

You should start the conversation on a neutral topic. This can be a query on whether there was any difficulty in finding the firm or with the travel route taken. More adventurously, you may feel like picking up some unusual aspect of the applicant's leisure time which you have gleaned from the CV. Do not try to monopolise the conversation; if the applicant is happy to discourse on something you can afford to give him/her the stage at this point. This will help him/her to feel more at ease and establish some self-confidence. Later on you may have to steer the comments along a route you have planned.

At some stage you need to get back to the task in hand. You can do this by explaining the purpose of the interview, how it will be conducted and whether your guest will be undertaking any tests or have an opportunity to visit the working area. Once these points are clarified you are ready to start the interview proper.

Question time

Try to avoid an atmosphere of interrogation.

You are now after evidence – facts that, it is to be hoped, you will be able to build up to form a file on the applicant and his/her suitability (or otherwise) for the job. Ideally, you should do this by trying to make the candidate forget that he/she is being interviewed at all. He/she should be encouraged to talk and answer questions on specific matters, the overall structure of which has been determined by you. A good way to start this is to pick an item from the application that may need clarifying. To introduce it, lead in with: 'There's something here I don't quite understand.' Note, it is *you* who doesn't understand. You are not suggesting that the content is confusing because of the writer – this could immediately put the interviewee down. You are simply not quite sure about a point and asking for it to be made clear.

We do not intend to list strings of clever, probing questions – other books have covered this in great detail. To be good at this you must have the questions off pat; dictating (or appearing to recite) a question will make applicants realise that they are being interrogated – a fact you are striving to avoid. Also, no two interviews are the same. You are confronting a stranger and neither of you knows what course the discussion will take.

A selection interview should be as personal as possible. Questions should follow each other naturally, individual queries arising out of an earlier answer. You are much more liable to extract useful information from an affable discussion than from a set of stereotyped questions to which the applicant may understandably feel there are stereotyped answers – and he/she doesn't know them!

Start with simple low-threat questions which demand fairly straightforward answers. Ask questions one at a time - you do not want to confuse your guest.

The delicate or difficult questions should be broached half way through the interview. This allows enough time for the candidate to have settled down and gained some self-confidence, and also ensures that any embarrassing exchange does not take place just before the technical interview. Examples in this category are: the reason he/she was dismissed from his/her last job, any domestic problem indicated by the application form or similar questions that have to be asked on personal circumstances.

Questions should cover all the areas usually listed on an application form or CV.

Activities and interests

Let candidate expand on his/her interests.

Don't forget to cover leisure interests and outside work activities. These often reveal characteristics about the job applicant which, with a little reasoning, can tell you something about his/her outlook on life and whether he/she will fit into the new job environment. If the subject interests them, job applicants are liable to talk freely and enthusiastically - you may even have a job restraining them!

Be on the lookout for interests that relate in some way to the job applied for. An electronics engineer who is also a radio 'ham' who builds his own equipment is obviously keen on this type of work. Taking part in a sport (as opposed to just observing it) generally indicates a willingness to mix and be competitive, even more so with team sports. Voluntary service in any capacity is a plus point, indicating motivation and empathy in what is now generally considered to be a material world. A correct code of behaviour can generally be assumed in the case of sincere religious affiliations.

Dangerous activities such as hang-gliding, rock climbing or stock car racing should command some consideration, especially if they are indulged in enthusiastically. The question must be asked: 'How much time is the candidate liable to spend in hospital or be otherwise incapacitated?'

An appreciable amount of time spent on stamp collecting or model building (unless relevant to the job) may also rouse speculation. These are often the pastimes of a 'loner' or introvert, which is fine if the job involves working alone but they should be regarded with concern if the job entails working as a team. The point to watch is the extent to which the applicant is taken up with the activity.

Techniques

Let the candidate speak.

Ideally, you should strive to contribute no more than a quarter of the total words in the verbal exchange. In fact the ratio will change gradually from the start of the meeting where you may be handling two-thirds of the conversation. Remember, you only learn facts by listening; and you can't listen while you're talking! As the interview proceeds, only an occasional prompting or new question or topic should come from you.

Be careful not to anticipate and finish a sentence. Always give your visitor time to complete an answer fully. Even when this appears to have ended, it is often wise to wait, silent and expectant, just in case the interviewee feels he/she has more information to give. Only when you consider the topic has been fully exhausted should you step in and introduce another subject.

Look for opportunities to delve deeper.

When you have gained more experience you will probably develop your own techniques for questioning. Remember, an interview is not an interrogation – ideally your questions should come out of a friendly discussion by two people on a given subject. You should always be on the lookout for an opportunity. A candidate may occasionally throw in a sentence that opens up a new field of information on just what makes him/her tick. You must recognise this and lead in straight away with: 'Oh, and how did this come about?' or some similar expression.

Avoid questions which invite 'Yes' or 'No' answers.

It shouldn't be too difficult to ensure that your questions are open-ended. You must learn to leave alone queries where an answer of either 'Yes' or 'No' is all that can be expected. When used to confirm something in an application form this type of exchange is a complete waste of valuable interviewing time.

Your function is to listen, observe and evaluate. The candidate must therefore be given ample opportunity to talk. You should show interest in what the job applicant has to say and encourage him/her to express him/herself. This can be done with a nod or a smile; verbal interjection should be kept to a minimum. Unless you need to direct the course of the questioning, your doing the talking contributes nothing. An exception, of course, is the time taken to tell your visitor about the company and the job. Try to maintain eye contact and lean forward occasionally to emphasise a point.

Note taking

You will have your check sheet to keep you on the straight and narrow. If sections are marked off as described in the last chapter (see pages 91-93), you will know the time taken already and the points that have still to be covered.

Avoid making notes when candidate is talking.

When you have to write down notes or comments, try to make the action inconspicuous. Avoid writing when comments or answers are being given or immediately after. This can unsettle the candidate and make him/her wonder what it was he/she just said that warrants recording. Try to develop the technique of making your comments on an answer while you are putting the next question.

Use key words when note taking.

Don't be too explicit in your notes. Wherever possible, key words should be used which will enable you to recall the topic immediately after the meeting.

Imparting information

One of the traditional routines of the job interview is to ask job applicants what they know of the company. They are presumably expected to spend time in the local library gleaning and memorising statistics about the firm they hope to join. This is still the routine in many organisations but it is so stereotyped that it is not to be recommended. It can only prove that applicants have spent time collecting the information. Rarely are they expected to relate their newly acquired knowledge. If the question: 'What, if anything, do you know of our company?' is posed by a personnel officer, the answer is frequently interrupted by the personnel officer taking over and giving a prepared statement on the subject. So why waste valuable interviewing time?

Tell the candidate about the job and the firm.

Part of your brief is to ensure that the job applicant is supplied with realistic data about the job and the working conditions. This is also a good time to explain points that you want to make about the firm. Some of this can be in leaflet or brochure form and simply handed over with comments on any item of significance.

The applicant should be left in no doubt as to what his /her tasks will be. From the job description you should fully describe these and give special mention of any unusual aspects of the work. Where possible, this can be related to the applicant's previous experience and thus suitability for the job. If a job description was not sent with the application form a copy should be given to the applicant.

You must also have information available on the conditions of employment and associated matters, such as hours of work, holiday entitlement and whether overtime will be required. Opportunities for training, promotion prospects and information on social or sports facilities should be covered.

Discussing salary.

The question of salary should also be introduced at this time. You will want to observe how the job applicant feels about the salary offered. This should be ascertained before the topic of fringe benefits (if any) is reached; if the candidate appears satisfied with the salary on offer, any additional emoluments will seem like a bonus.

Candidate's questions

Before the end of the session you should offer the candidate the opportunity to ask questions.

You should be prepared to answer questions about the company pension scheme or other matters that you may have neglected to cover earlier. Do not be too critical of the type of questions - they may be important to the questioner. But you will surely make a note about applicants who only ask about salary or ask irrelevant questions on the benefits of working for the firm. One question you should be prepared for is: 'What happened to the last person in the job?'

When no questions are asked.

By this time you should have developed an easy rapport with your guest and only a little prompting should be necessary. If no questions are forthcoming you may have covered your induction session so well that none is needed. But this is unlikely. Job applicants who ask no questions at this stage have either already made up their mind that they are not interested in the job or have an unusually low intellect and cannot think of anything to ask. If they appear to have great difficulty in finding something to ask about a new job you are perhaps justified in asking yourself: 'Are they really for me?'

Qualifications

Ask to see proof of qualifications.

Where the candidate has stated on the application form that qualifications are held, sight of these should be requested and brief details entered on the interview check sheet. Where the candidate has neglected to bring evidence of the qualifications you should ask why. You can then decide whether you need to ask your visitor to send copies on to you as soon as possible.

Salary

For the small firm the salary on offer may be restricted by the overall budget and not open to negotiation. In this case it is as well to state the salary in the job advertisement and thus assume that applicants are willing to accept this figure.

It is likely that a promising candidate will try to have the salary increased but this should not be acceded to easily, if at all. You will no doubt have spent some time on determining a policy on staff remuneration and violating this could jeopardise relations with existing staff.

Fringe benefits can enhance salary value.

It is useful to have a few benefits available to serve as part of a package. They can be introduced as incentives if the interviewee appears to be wavering because the salary offered is insufficient. You should also be in a position to explain the amount and frequency of any merit payments.

It is quite usual nowadays to agree a starting salary with the proviso that it will be increased (or renegotiated) after three months.

School and college leavers

Interviewing first-time employees needs a little more care. Despite the often-heard criticism of modern youth being irresponsible, selfish and undisciplined, many lack self-confidence and, ironically, they are the ones who are serious about trying to obtain their first position. It is possible that their only serious relationships with adults have been restricted to parents and teachers.

Initially, your aim is the same as with other candidates – to try to make them feel at ease as soon as possible – but it will be more difficult because there is an age difference.

Try to relate to their environment.

You will need to relate to their activities, current way of life, likes and dislikes. This can be done, even if you have never heard of their favourite pop group! Your chief difficulty will be to ensure that you do not appear to patronise them.

The trouble is that you have so little to start with. There may be something on the application form that catches your eye; if so, seize it with the knowledge of developing the subject and possibly diverting on to other topics. If there isn't, you will have to be content with discussing school or college achievements and activities. You may need to work at it but a friendly approach and a genuine effort to listen to what they have to say should pay off.

You may form the impression that the interviewee is permanently on the defence and reluctant to reveal much about him/herself. This is invariably because he/she feels totally out of his/her depth. You have somehow to throw a life-line - even if it means going back to basics and asking if he/she enjoyed school!

If you can break through, you will need to steer the conversation round so that you can evaluate him/her as you would any other candidate. Is there a stable family relationship? If he/she is living away from home, how does he/she manage?

Difficult encounters.

If you are unfortunate enough to encounter a stone-wall, you may be forced to accept that the applicant is not for you. Ability or experience cannot be determined but remember the other important parameter - compatibility. If you are unable to bring the candidate out and develop some rapport in a relatively casual environment, how will it be when you are trying to instil some aspect of the job?

Graduate applicants

This type of applicant will be a few years older and will probably have lived away from home; you could, in fact, be meeting a mature person. The only thing lacking could be work experience, although that may have been gained doing vacation jobs.

Ascertain how vacations were spent.

Again, you will have to search for information or a topic and try to expand on it. One possibility is how they occupied their time on vacation and why. If it was some form of work, no matter how menial, it will be useful. This type of applicant will probably have some idea of what he/she wants to do in the future and it may be interesting to hear how he/she is able to express this.

In the role of interviewer, you must always be on the lookout for facts and with both the graduate and the college leaver these will only be academic achievements. Although a degree speaks for itself, the sixth-form years - assuming some time was spent in this environment - could be interesting as they will presumably show progress to A levels. Alternatively, if the applicant has come up the hard way with a spell of employment before going to a polytechnic or university, this should be something to discuss.

The conversation is only of superficial value in all these cases. It may be confined to interests and even personal likes and dislikes, but it will generally be enough to enable you to form an opinion of the applicant. It is up to you to develop the encounter and progress along lines that may throw up some pointers as to the applicant's qualities, if any, and what makes him/her tick.

The unemployed

Some empathy should be shown to the unemployed person seeking a position. He/she may feel at a disadvantage compared with other job applicants and you must try to allay any fears and put across the fact that he/she is being treated equally and as seriously as any other candidate called to interview.

There is no reason why the matter should be discussed but equally there is no reason to hide or ignore the facts. You must first establish the reason why the candidate left his/her last firm. You should not try to avoid the issue – it is far better to use the circumstances in another context; for instance: 'What sort of planning have you used in your job search?' or 'How have you occupied your time during this period?' Both are direct questions and should ascertain what approach was taken and if the forced leisure time was spent usefully. Another harmless question is: 'Did you maintain contact with colleagues at your old firm?' These questions are relatively easy to answer and should not embarrass the applicant. They can help to build self-confidence during the remainder of the interview.

Use tactful questions.

The technical interview

This is the second stage in the interviewing programme. When closing the first interview you should let the candidate know when a decision is likely to be made. Try to ascertain if he/she is still interested in the job. If there are any doubts you may be able to clarify the issue before the candidate leaves.

Handing your visitor over to the second assessor.

You will then either take your guest to the second assessor or arrange for him/her to be collected from your office. The former is to be recommended as it promotes a human image and enables you to introduce the candidate to the next interviewer.

You will have already discussed with the second interviewer what is expected and, it is hoped, asked him/her to suggest what form the second stage will take. It should be made as informal as possible. Assuming that there have been no ominous developments in the interview so far, the candidate should be feeling fairly relaxed by now.

The second interview should use the techniques employed when the candidate first arrived - a friendly greeting followed by some chat on a neutral topic.

The new interviewer will be interested in the same things as you: the candidate's ability to undertake the job tasks and his/her compatibility with the rest of the workforce in that section. Some form of test may have been planned to assess the former.

Selection tests

These may be to do with the trade or profession concerned where the candidate is asked to perform tasks similar to those he/she would undertake in the job. On the other hand, some type of psychometric test may be used.

Trade tests

Simple attainment tests are usually possible in most jobs. An applicant for a secretarial position would be asked to undertake a typing and/or shorthand test, or be given an audio tape to transcribe.

Always give candidate a trial run of the test.

Allow for a warm up session before the typing test proper. And if you intend checking a typing speed make your observation inconspicuous by saying, 'Start when you like', and noting the starting time on your watch. You should prepare a page of text beforehand from which you can determine the speed attained.

Some form of work test is essential.

The technical interviewer should always introduce some form of work test. This may range from, say, going over a circuit diagram with an electronic technician down to a few casual questions on apparatus used in the working routine. Many jobs now involve working with computers and it can be enlightening to ask the candidates what they know of this subject. Some may reveal sufficient interest to have delved into programming and this obviously shows an enquiring and industrious mind.

Not to take this opportunity of evaluating a candidate's practical knowledge of the job could prove very embarrassing if he/she is later found to be incapable of doing the job.

Psychometric tests

Mostly used for executive level posts.

These are designed to evaluate a person's in-built characteristics and discover his/her rating in either general intelligence, personality or aptitude for a certain type of work. However, they are only generally suitable for high-level jobs and care must be taken to ensure that the candidate is able to understand what is required and up to taking the test.

The use of this type of test is not universally accepted and there are doubts about the validity of the results. As might be expected, certain software applications have been developed for DIY psychological testing.

Source of information on occupational testing.

The Institute of Personnel Management has published a code on occupational testing for employers considering the use of tests and this fully covers the subject. Copies can be obtained free from them on IPM House, Camp Road, Wimbledon, London SW19 4UX; 081-946 9100.

Executive level applicants

For supervisory and middle management positions a different approach is needed. Here you are trying to determine leadership qualities and future commitment to the company and you should therefore attempt to steer the conversation in order to ascertain the extent of these attributes.

One way of doing this is to introduce a few difficult or tricky situations that could arise in the job. They could range from the handling of a problem with the labour force to a logistical matter where, say, there has been a serious breakdown in the supply of materials. Problems can be simulated and put to the applicants with the question: 'What would you do in these circumstances?'

There need be no set answers to any of the problems. You will be more interested in the approach taken and whether the candidates look at the problem from all angles and appreciate the implications. Do they rush in full of enthusiasm or pause for a moment to think? Are they completely overwhelmed? It may be useful to jot down a few key words here to remind you of the answers given. This will help when you are making your final assessment of the candidates.

Departure

Be courteous when saying goodbye.

The second interviewer will generally be responsible for escorting the job applicant off the premises, although in some circumstances you may wish to do this yourself. With a promising candidate it is useful as you can find out how he/she felt about the second part of the evaluation.

The candidate should be made to feel that his/her visit was well worthwhile and that you, as a prospective employer, know all you need to know about his/her suitability for the job. It is not advisable to give any indication about a candidate's eligibility, although occasionally candidates sound out their prospects by saying they are expecting a result from an interview with another firm. You should not commit yourself at this stage.

If aspiring employees can leave you with the knowledge that they have been given a realistic hearing, you have done your job well. It is a bonus if they also feel that your firm would be a nice one to work for!

◀ CHAPTER 8 ▶

MAKING THE SELECTION

You should now have all the information you need to make your final selection. From this point the procedure will consist of:

- completing a selection rating check sheet (as soon as possible after the interview);
- comparing each applicant's assessment with the person specification (and job analysis);
- producing a shortlist of three or four suitable candidates;
- deciding who is to be offered the job.

Documenting facts

The progress of the recruitment programme is documented on the record of recruitment form. Accurate, more detailed records of facts are required for all candidates from the interview stage onwards to the final selection and should include the results of any tests.

Confidentiality essential.

All information gathered and commented on must be treated in the strictest confidence. Access to this data must be confined to those directly involved in the programme and responsible for making the final selection.

Any factors that make the selectors decide that a candidate is not suitable must be especially well documented, if necessary by separate reports accompanying the interview and selection ratings form. This is essential in case the decision not to employ is challenged by an unsuccessful candidate and a complaint made to a tribunal under a discriminatory clause in the current legislation.

Selection rating check

This should be undertaken as soon as possible after the interview – preferably on the same day but certainly on the following morning. If you leave it any later you may forget some point. You will (or should have) made notes and used key words to identify a candidate's significant attributes. But no one is infallible. A point could have been missed – or even disregarded because it was so significant at the time that you were sure you would remember it. Candidates are assessed using the selection rating form, an example of which is given on page 112.

Assemble information in one folder.

As well as the selection rating form you should retain all other notes, letters, interview checklist, application form (and CV if any) in a folder. In this way you have all the information on the applicant to hand.

Even if you have almost unknowingly singled out an eminently suitable candidate you should not make any decision at this stage that will exclude other applicants. The selection procedure will enable you to produce a list of eligible candidates in order of suitability. The ideal candidate may ultimately refuse your offer and you then have a quick replacement on hand. Also, an evaluated list of applicants is useful for future vacancies.

Rating system.

You will now have to decide a rating between 1 and 6 against the entries on the form. This will range from totally unsuitable (1) to eminently suitable (6). Note that there is no halfway mark – this ensures that you do not take the easy way out and give an 'average' rating when making the assessment. Even for borderline cases you must make a decision and come out marginally one way or the other – for or against the candidate. Use the space to the right for additional comments.

No weighting is suggested on this occasion. Weighting was useful in the early stages when the applicant had not been interviewed, but having now met and talked with the person being evaluated you should have formed some opinions which will have subjective weighting.

Use interview check sheet to your ratings.

Do not forget to use the interview check sheet and note the comments you made during the meeting. In particular, you should spend some time evaluating the list of attributes on the lower part of this form. You may feel like changing your original rating in this section – or making an assessment which had not been possible previously because there were insufficient facts.

Selection rating form

APPLICANT ☐ JOB APPLIED FOR ☐

ASSESSOR ☐ INTERVIEW DATE ☐

Person specification	1 ☐ ☐ ☐ ☐ ☐ ☐ ☐ ☐ ☐ ☐ 10
Experience	1 ☐ ☐ ☐ ☐ ☐ ☐ 6
Education	1 ☐ ☐ ☐ ☐ ☐ ☐ 6
Stability	1 ☐ ☐ ☐ ☐ ☐ ☐ 6
Compatibility	1 ☐ ☐ ☐ ☐ ☐ ☐ 6
Maturity	1 ☐ ☐ ☐ ☐ ☐ ☐ 6
Motivation	1 ☐ ☐ ☐ ☐ ☐ ☐ 6
Suitability	1 ☐ ☐ ☐ ☐ ☐ ☐ 6
Communication skills	1 ☐ ☐ ☐ ☐ ☐ ☐ 6
Leadership	1 ☐ ☐ ☐ ☐ ☐ ☐ 6
Loyalty	1 ☐ ☐ ☐ ☐ ☐ ☐ 6
General impression	1 ☐ ☐ ☐ ☐ ☐ ☐ 6

Comment

Suitable for employment 1 ☐ ☐ ☐ ☐ ☐ ☐ ☐ ☐ ☐ ☐ 10

Assessor's position ....

Assessor's signature .... Date ....

Rating a candidate's suitability

You now have to work your way through the list and allocate a rating by ticking the appropriate box. The following notes may help you to arrive at a realistic assessment.

Person specification

How nearly does candidate meet person specification?

This is the one subject where you are asked to allocate points out of 10; 6 is too few to give a true assessment.

Here you must have the person specification for the job to hand. From the documentary information held and items gleaned during the interview you must allocate a figure (out of 10) which describes how well the candidate meets the criteria of the job specification. It is suggested that to qualify for serious consideration, candidates will require a rating of at least 6.

Experience

Will training be needed?

This covers job-related skills and knowledge and how easy it will be for the applicant to move into the vacant position. Does the experience claimed fit in with that required for the greater part of the job? How much further training will be required for a candidate to take over the tasks fully? To what extent has he/she kept up with modern techniques? Basically, what is his/her current level of skills relevant to the work being carried out in your organisation?

Especially in technical positions, it is rare for an applicant to be able to walk into another position without some form of induction training. The amount required should be clear after evaluating the job analysis and the person specification. You have to decide what the costs will be in time, money and training resources to carry out this induction. You must also assess the attitude and motivation of the candidate for this process. Does he/she seem enthusiastic about further training and is he/she the type who will benefit from it?

Education

More relevant to younger candidates.

To what extent does the applicant's education and training make him/her suitable for the job? Are qualifications held in the specific subject?

This assessment is less important for older applicants where experience of the work is often of more value than qualifications.

Will he/she stay in the job?

Stability

Does the applicant's record show a string of jobs over a relatively short period? What, if any, were the excuses for this? Have you any facts or information that make you feel the candidate will move on shortly?

There are also other aspects that will show the degree of a candidate's stability. Was the passage through school or college systematic, or did it involve a change of direction resulting in an attainment that was less than that originally anticipated? Did the candidate drop out of a course before achieving the aimed-for certificate? The question to be asked is whether the candidate has a record of not finishing what is started. On a more personal note, has the candidate been divorced or separated? It may seem unfair to assess suitability on this but there could be repercussions liable to affect job performance.

Compatibility

How will he/she get on with other people?

Apart from the candidate getting along with existing staff, the question must also be asked: 'Will the current workforce accept and get along with the applicant?' During your one-to-one meeting did you have any misgivings about the candidate's compatibility? Did it appear that he/she had difficulty in relations with people generally? Again, going further back, was there any indication of difficulties with fellow students or teachers?

How does the candidate seem to get on with members of his/her own family? Does he/she live at home, share a flat or house with others or elect to live alone?

If the work is of a solitary nature this aspect may not be as important, but it is still worth thinking about the consequences.

Maturity

This is difficult to assess but can be a problem for any employer. Everyone shows immaturity to some extent and the difficulty is in deciding to what degree it is acceptable.

Some pointers to immaturity.

Immaturity is recognisable as selfishness, lack of self-discipline, boastfulness, a tendency to avoid responsibility and yet an attempt to enforce often unreasonable tasks on subordinates. Lack of self-control and an unwillingness to undertake unpleasant tasks are further examples. Trying to avoid admitting anything embarrassing or unpleasant are other attributes of the immature and this may have been revealed during the interview.

This type of immaturity has little to do with age. There is a grey area between mature and immature people and the prospective employer must decide whether the degree of immaturity detected is acceptable in the person engaged for a particular type of work.

Motivation

Assessment of candidate's initiative in the job.

This covers an inclination to work and can be traced back to school or college days. It can appear as being eager to progress, show initiative and possibly gain promotion - an inclination to be actively productive and not prepared just to sit and wait to be told to do something.

Ideally, you are looking for someone who is self-motivated but not driven by financial reward alone. A person who can show a record of motivation and a 'get up and go' attitude is worthy of serious consideration even if there is a shortfall in other factors.

Suitability

Will candidate be able to adapt to any changes in the job - different from his/her early experience?

Here you must assess the applicant's suitability for the work on a more general basis. Is the type of work similar to that already being performed? Will the applicant be able to handle an appreciable change; for instance, from a regular 9 to 5 environment to perhaps shift working? If the post offered requires technical knowledge but also some salesmanship, has the applicant any sales training? Does he/she fully realise the implications of dealing with customers?

If the difference in the work is appreciable you will have decided whether the applicant is worth considering earlier in the selection programme. However, you now have to evaluate the attributes and confirm that the differences are within the capabilities of the applicant. It boils down to whether he/she is able to adapt and take the new environment in his/her stride.

Executive positions

Additional considerations for candidates for high-level positions.

The attributes noted above should be considered in applicants for all positions in the workforce. However, when the candidate is seeking a position in management there are other factors to evaluate.

The fact that the applicant has held a senior position previously will appear on the application form and CV and, provided there is an acceptable reason for leaving, it can be assumed that some leadership qualities have been acquired.

It is more difficult to assess a candidate who has no such experience and seeks to make his/her first move up to an executive position. He/she may have the potential to become a good manager but you have to examine the facts carefully. It is reasonable to ask if a senior position was sought in the applicant's previous firm, and if not why not?

There are obviously qualities that must be evaluated in any seeker of a responsible and supervisory position.

Communication skills

Will candidate be able to communicate upwards as well as to subordinate staff?

Will the applicant be able to communicate effectively? Are writing skills adequate (judged in part from the application form) to pass on information to others? What are the oral qualities of the applicant? Can he/she express him/herself sufficiently well to get the message across to the workforce on the shop floor as well as to inhabitants of the board room - even when under pressure?

Although communication skills can be taught, the greater part of this technique is inherent and learnt by experience, possibly during college days. People who show very little aptitude or appreciation of the need for good communication are unlikely to function well as managers.

Leadership

Will the applicant inspire confidence in subordinates? This is perhaps the most important attribute of a manager. Without it, respect is lost and the whole work routine may suffer.

Responsibilities of leadership.

Does the candidate enjoy being a leader and fully realise the responsibilities? Has a supervisory position been held for an acceptable length of time? Will the applicant be able to reach a decision after assessing all aspects of a situation? Is it clear that part of the leadership role involves relating to others and, on occasions, working alongside the rest of the staff to accomplish a result?

It is worth checking to see if the candidate held any positions of responsibility at school or college. Was there an inclination to take the lead in activities? Also to be considered when assessing this quality is whether the candidate's leadership will be accepted by others.

Loyalty

In your judgement, to what extent will the applicant be prepared to serve the company?

Determining degrees of loyalty.

Some aspects of loyalty will have been determined during the interviewing process, especially if a situation has been described that allows the loyalty factor to be assessed. Applicants who denigrate their previous employer, or other organisations they are connected with, are unlikely to give unrestricted support to you as a future employer.

Need to support the team.

You are looking for someone who seeks to identify closely with the company and become a member of the team, someone who has supported family and friends during difficult periods. Ideally, you need someone who will put the company before self or family, but not to a ridiculous degree. The extent to which this can be judged should be entered on your scale.

General impression

This chiefly refers to the appearance and impact of the candidates and what your first reaction was when you first met them.

Did they take the trouble to put on a suit or otherwise smarten themselves up in spite of the fact that the work itself will be done in jeans or overalls? The fact that the man or woman may have been wearing what, in the interviewer's opinion, is too much jewellery or scent may or may not be relevant to the job but you must consider the person's attitude in wearing them - likewise with an outrageous hairstyle. Was it to show independence, make a stand or establish a precedent? No matter what job is sought, there is an acceptable norm for attending interviews (if they are to have any chance of being fruitful). To violate this can hardly warrant a plus point.

Here we must consider the question of alcohol. Alcohol on the breath is quite discernible but it is often difficult to decide whether the amount consumed has been a social half pint or, to use a more descriptive phrase, a skin-full. The time of day can be significant as many enjoy a lunch-time drink. However, you are justified in asking if the candidate imbibed because:

- he/she usually did at this time; or
- he/she felt it necessary to have some Dutch courage; or
- he/she could not stop themselves doing so.

Even the first option, however innocent, is worthy of criticism as it implies that the candidate is unaware that his/her breath may cause concern. Further, if there was an awareness, he/she was apparently not prepared to forgo a drink on this occasion. Even the sweetest smelling candidate may have a problem in this area but you may only find this out later. You would surely be tempting providence to accept a person when symptoms of the fact are evident and flaunted at the interview!

Making the selection

The remainder of the entries on the selection rating form refer directly to each applicant's rating for the post.

In the 'Comment' area you must summarise your thoughts on the applicant. Strengths and weaknesses are evaluated and, if any single point warrants mention, you record it.

Consider only important facts.

When assessing a candidate's suitability, do not be influenced too much by relatively unimportant strengths (or weaknesses). Concentrate on points that will have a significant effect on the job on offer.

As far as possible you should try to be objective but on some issues this will be impossible. The X factor inevitably appears again. Here, you are inadvertently making a subjective comment which is a response to your intuition. The content of this section must support the rating in the scale below.

The 'Suitability for employment' section is a scale from 1 to 10 in which you make your final assessment on the applicant. The scale will range from totally unsuitable for this post (1) to eminently suitable for this post (which could be between 8 and 10).

Note that you are not making the final decision at this stage. You are recording the degree of suitability of the person being assessed. This assessment will be compared with that of the other candidates.

The final decision must remain pending until all candidates have been evaluated, all information has been considered and recorded, and a rating given. The rating is the important issue and whether it is used now or in a few weeks' time is irrelevant.

Arithmetical grading should support general view.

The final selection is the candidate with the highest score in the ratings. This sounds glib but if each attribute has been carefully evaluated and graded numerically this should indicate the best applicant. The arithmetical answer simply provides a clear decision. Where a strong indication of the best candidate has materialised during the routine of interviews, the candidate's numerical rating should endorse this. If it doesn't you will need to check any suspect areas.

Second assessor's opinion.

There is no reason why the second assessor (or technical interviewer) should not go through a separate selection rating form; a second opinion is always useful. The forms should be attached to each other. This person's interview checklist should at least be used during your final considerations. If there is disagreement on the ultimate choice, the ratings of the attributes on the selection rating form will provide a good basis for discussion and resolution.

Inability to reach a decision

In your efforts to make a selection you will have evaluated all the information and have been guided by facts on paper as well as observations during interview. In spite of this you may still be unable to reach a decision. The deliberation will most likely be on the final selection from a group of candidates, but may also be because few appeared to reach the suitable standard.

Take time to review each candidate a second time.

You must not let the urgency or pressure of the situation influence you. Giving an unwarranted high rating after another look at the selection rating form is unrealistic.

In some cases the situation can be resolved by a second interview. If this seems likely, by all means arrange it. It may mean deciding between two candidates or a re-run of all those interviewed. In either case it is preferable to implementing a fresh recruitment programme.

Use of references

References have been included here because they can be used as an aid to the selection process. However, in most cases the request for written references is made during the final stages of the recruitment procedure, usually after an offer for the job has been sent out.

References serve two basic functions:

- to verify information already given in a CV or application form;
- to extract further details of a person's character. In this context they are used to confirm (or otherwise) an interviewer's impressions of a candidate, formed during an interview.

The taking-up of references is usually a formality but they can occasionally make a valuable contribution to the selection process. This is especially so in the case of the telephone reference which is mentioned on page 124.

Personal references

Usually of little value.

These are written by friends or prominent people on the virtues of the person they refer to. The writers often go on so rapturously about the applicant's attributes that you may feel they have been dictated by him/her! They are valueless; who would realistically offer a personal reference if it did not paint the subject in the best possible colours?

Occasionally, this type of personal reference will be forwarded after a request – when only a name and address is wanted. The recruiter must ensure that at least one reference originates from a postholder of authority at the applicant's previous or most recent employer.

Unsolicited testimonials

This type of credential is occasionally presented as an unsolicited reference where it has obviously been solicited by the subject. It is usually headed: To whom it may concern. Again, little or no credence should be afforded to this type of reference when submitted to support an application for permanent employment.

Solicited references

These are written reports or completed questionnaires which have been compiled, usually by the subject's previous company, at the request of a prospective employer.

Limitations of solicited references.

Previous employers are usually wary of providing detrimental references on unsatisfactory employees. They will also not be keen on giving satisfactory references when the performance of the past employee has been below standard. This is understandable as in both cases they would be in a precarious position should the recently departed employee decide to take action about unfair dismissal. This shows just how difficult it is to expect a reliable reference in today's job recruitment scene.

There is no obligation in law to provide a reference, but most firms are prepared to do so as they realise that they themselves often require this information and know it can be important. Refusal to give a reference can automatically be regarded as a condemnation of the previous employee.

Many government departments confine their references to a statement confirming the fact that a person was employed by them for a given length of time. However, this type of reference from a commerical firm should be regarded with suspicion and as an attempt to be non-committal. In these circumstances it would make sense to telephone the writer to discover the reason for this.

Use a questionnaire.

If you simply write to one of the referees asking for a reference you will probably receive an assortment of replies. The referees quoted by

Example A: Request for a reference

To ....

....

....

Dear

Your name has been given to us as a reference by the person named below who has applied for a permanent position with our company. Would you please provide the information requested and return this form in the stamped addressed envelope provided. Your replies will be treated in the strictest confidence.

Many thanks for your assistance.

Works Manager

APPLICANT'S NAME ....

JOB APPLIED FOR ....

Date engaged by you .... Date of leaving .... Final salary £ ....

What position did he/she hold in your employment? ....

What were the main duties? ....

What was the reason for leaving? ....

While employed by you was he/she:

honest and sober? ....

a good time keeper? ....

a reliable worker? ....

Is there any reason you feel he/she should not be employed in the above position?

Have you any general comments you care to make?

Signed .... Position .... Date ....

Example B: Request for a reference

Ref:

Date

Mr J V Robinson
North End Fabrications Limited
Unit 3B
North End Industrial Estate
Wolverhampton
Post code

Dear Mr Robinson

REFERENCE – HAROLD BUNSON

The above named has applied to us for a position as Site Project Engineer and given your name as a reference.

We would appreciate your comments on Mr Bunson's suitability for this post and to assist this we enclose a questionnaire. Could you please complete this and return it to us in the attached pre-paid envelope.

Thank you very much for your assistance in this matter.

Yours sincerely
for AVON ENGINEERING LIMITED

Brian J Mitchell
Technical Director

Enc: Reference questionnaire

Reference questionnaire

APPLICANT'S NAME ....

JOB APPLIED FOR ....

Please provide the information requested below. All comments will be treated in the strictest confidence.

	Particulars supplied by applicant	Your agreement (or comments)
Job title		
Main duties		
Dates of employment		
Salary on leaving		
Reason for leaving		

While in your employment was he/she:	YES, tick	NO, please comment
• honest and sober?	☐	
• a good time keeper?	☐	
• a reliable worker?	☐	
• able to get along with supervisors and colleagues?	☐	
• healthy and apparently fit?	☐	

Is he/she, in your opinion, suitable for the post applied for? YES/NO Would you re-employ him/her? YES/NO

Are there any problems it would be useful for us to know about?

Are there any other comments you care to make?

Signed .... Position .... Date ....

candidates on an application form may not have known them very well and be non-committal in the reply. By far the most fruitful method is to send a questionnaire. A manager can then pass it to the supervisor of the recent employee for completion.

Two examples are given on pages 121–23. One consists of questions set out on a form which is part of the letter. This will suffice for the majority of staff. The second example consists of a separate letter which introduces a further page containing the questions. This is suitable for more senior positions.

In all cases courtesy is essential. You are usually imposing on a busy person's work time and expecting him/her to devote time to answering your queries. It is of nuisance value to the addressee but it is important to you that you obtain the information.

A quick method of obtaining a reference.

Telephone references

This is a practical and speedy way of obtaining a reference and can often be the best approach when facts are needed urgently. Previous employers are generally more relaxed and liable to reveal more over the telephone than they would in a letter. They can certainly be more truthful and this type of communication has the advantage that the narrator's voice and manner can often give some interpretation of his/her opinion of your candidate.

You should make the most of the opportunity. Arguably, your best chance to assess the applicant is during the interview, but you only have an hour. Here you have the chance to speak to someone who has first-hand knowledge of the candidate in a working environment, probably for some months. This will be one of the few opportunities to obtain a realistic appraisal of the applicant by a person in the same position as you – an employer.

Prepare questions beforehand.

Because it is usually a short procedure the telephone method can often be used early in the recruitment programme, say, immediately prior to deciding on a shortlist to interview. But it can also help in the final selection process and occasionally reveal a factor that decides the final choice. It works best when a checklist of questions to be put to the previous employer is made out beforehand. These must be short and capable of being answered without reference to files. It is often a good opportunity to put one of the most poignant of all questions: 'Would you re-employ him/her?'

An example of a checklist when using the telephone reference

Record of telephone reference

NAME OF APPLICANT

Person contacted

Company | Tel No

Opening remark:

Mr/Ms/Mrs/Miss .... has applied to us for a position and I wonder if you could verify some information he/she has given us?

Tick if true

What position did he/she hold?

What were the main duties?

How long was he/she with you?

What was the reason for leaving?

He/she has stated his/her final salary was £ | Is this true?

	YES	NO
Could he/she work without supervision?	☐	☐
Did work results compare favourably with others?	☐	☐
Were there any domestic or financial problems?	☐	☐
Did any hobbies or other activcities affect his/her work?	☐	☐
Would you employ him/her again?	☐	☐

Closing remark

Thank you very much for your co-operation M...
I can assure you this information will be treated in the strictest confidence.

Signature of caller .... Date ....

procedure is shown on page 125. Note that all the spaces must be filled in before starting the call. This information can be obtained from the CV or application form.

Limitations of telephone reference.

The telephone reference can never take the place of the standard written procedure owing to the difficulty of maintaining an authentic record - a bank of audiotapes is hardly practicable. Its effectiveness is also limited by the responsiveness of whoever is questioned. The person who is questioned may be averse to divulging information over the telephone - and you have to be sure that you are speaking to a person of responsibility in the firm. But in many ways, references by telephone can make a useful contribution, if only to support the more drawn-out procedure of obtaining a reference by letter.

◀ CHAPTER 9 ▶

RECRUITMENT

After deciding who is to be offered the job you can progress to the final stage of recruitment. Initially this consists of sending the offer letter and continuing with associated administrative tasks.

Making the offer

Contents of offer letter.

The proposed salary and benefits of the post will have been discussed with the candidate during the interview. The successful applicant's availability may also be known and a provisional start date agreed. However, these facts have only been broached verbally and it is necessary to set them down in writing so that both the candidate and the company fully understand the terms of employment. This is done in a letter offering the job.

Overall, the letter should contain:

Checklist for letter offering employment.

- the offer of the job, stating the job title;
- the salary to be paid;
- the conditions of employment pertaining to the job. This can refer to a schedule which lists the conditions in detail;
- any probationary period to be worked;
- any restrictive conditions that apply, i.e. the appointment being made subject to the receipt of satisfactory references and attendance for (and satisfactory completion of) a medical examination if this is considered necessary;
- a reply slip (which may be part of the letter) on which the candidate

Ref:

Date

Mr B L Ferguson
12 Manor Drive
Hayton
Northampton
Post code

Dear Mr Ferguson

With regard to your recent visit to our offices we are pleased to offer you the position of Senior Sales Assistant at a salary of £14,500 per annum.

The conditions of employment are as set down in the attached schedule. You will initially be employed for a probationary period of three months during which time your employment may be terminated by one week's notice on either side.

The offer is subject to your passing a medical examination [if required] and the receipt of satisfactory references.

If you wish to accept our offer please sign one copy of this letter and return it. Would you also indicate the date on which you will be available to start.

I look forward to hearing from you.

Yours sincerely

John Frobisher
Divisional Manager

- -

I accept the offer of employment of the terms detailed above and would be prepared to commence work on . . .

Signed .... Date ....

confirms acceptance of the post together with all the conditions and advises a start date.

If you have not already done so, it will be necessary to state that you intend to obtain references from the names put forward earlier and request confirmation that this process can go ahead.

It is unlikely that the letter will cover all aspects of the terms of the employment but it does in itself form part of the contract. Where a further document contains important aspects of the contract of employment the letter should specifically refer to it.

Enclose other contract terms with the letter.

It is unnecessary to include an expiry date of the job offer. It is assumed that the candidate will respond quickly, but if a week passes with no acknowledgement it would be wise to telephone the person to ask if he/she is still interested in the post.

An example of a typical letter is shown on page 128. An original and one copy of the letter should be sent. This enables the candidate to retain proof of acceptance.

Job offers, or discussions on the final stages leading to an offer, should never be made by telephone. Remember, a verbal contract is legally binding and agreements reached verbally could lead to problems if, for any reason, they were misinterpreted. Job offers must be in writing.

Unsuccessful candidates

Writing to unsuccessful candidates.

When a selection has been made, unsuccessful candidates should be advised before the recruitment process continues. An exception might be where you delay telling your second choice for the post – until your prime candidate has accepted the offer. In general, many candidates will have applied to, and are probably in the process of being evaluated by, other employers. Delays in notifying them of their rejection could affect their consideration of other offers.

Much the same procedures for rejection are used as for those applicants who did not justify an interview. This time you will have spent an hour or so talking to the person you are about to reject and have an idea of how this will be taken. You should, however, still be wary of giving any reason for the rejection.

Communication should be by letter. There may have been an arrangement for you to advise a candidate by telephone but this should be avoided. Depending on your appraisal of the person involved, you should, however, be prepared to make a guarded comment about the

Avoid discussing reasons on telephone.

Ref:

Date

Mr J Richardson
143 Surtees Street
Leamington Spa
Post code

Dear Mr Richardson

VACANCY – SENIOR ACCOUNTS CLERK

Thank you for attending an interview for the above position.

After carefully evaluating your application I am sorry to have to tell you that we are unable to offer you a post on this occasion.

However, we should like to keep your details on file and will contact you again should a similar vacancy occur in the future.

Thank you for the interest you have shown in the company.

Yours sincerely
for ACME TRADING COMPANY LIMITED

Philip Brown
Divisional Manager

reason for failure over the telephone. It is possible that this could help the rejected candidate to reappraise the job-hunting procedure and strengthen his/her approach when applying for other jobs.

As the applicant reached the interview stage there is every reason for you to keep the details on file and you should state this in your letter. An example is given on page 130.

The letter is a refusal and nothing can change this. But by replying as soon as possible you will avoid having to give the unwelcome decision over the telephone. And by being courteous you have at least tried to project an image of a company that it would have been nice to work for.

Qualifications

Checking of qualifications.

Qualifications should be checked, if this has not already been done. This is particularly important where there is a statutory requirement that these qualifications are held by the person undertaking the job.

Requesting proof when not previously seen.

When not seen previously during the interview, photocopies of the relevant qualifications should be forwarded by the candidate, or proof of membership of a professional body by showing that the current year's subscription has been paid, if this is considered relevant. If there is any doubt about the candidate's status, the yearbook for the particular profession should be checked or a query addressed to the relevant examining body.

Sending for references

The acquiring of references can often be a nuisance to the recruiter, but they are a necessary adjunct to finalising the recruiting process. It can be frustrating to be held up because of the non-return of satisfactory references and some thought should be given as to avoiding this.

Some delay is acceptable when there is a proviso in the offer of employment stating that it is subject to: 'the receipt of satisfactory references', but this is not a particularly good way of doing things. This method can cause problems if the candidate is well into the initial month of service before a reference is received which makes you, as responsible for the recruitment, have doubts about the wisdom of continuing the employment.

The seeking of references cannot realistically be rushed as there is little point in asking for written references until an offer is about to be made, or at least until a shortlist of candidates has been drawn up.

The writing of references appears to be viewed with trepidation by some people and many are reluctant to put pen to paper, but large firms with personnel departments are geared to undertake this administrative chore.

Advise candidate during interview that references will be asked for.

In some cases your request for a reference may come as a surprise because the candidate has not warned his chosen referee to expect the approach. This should be clarified during the interview when the fact that references will be required should be brought up, and the candidate informed that any names put forward should be made aware that they will at some time be asked for references. You must emphasise it will be assumed that the referees will be willing to do this.

The referees' inconvenience should be kept to a minimum and the exercise made as painless as possible by providing a one-page questionnaire (see pages 121–23) and, of course, enclosing a stamped addressed envelope for the reply.

In extreme cases it may be necessary to inform the applicant that there has been no response to requests for a reference. In these circumstances he/she should be asked to contact the chosen referee in an effort to prompt a reply or, alternatively, offer further names who are prepared to support the applicant. If this has to be done it naturally reflects on the judgement of the aspiring candidate in selecting those particular referees in the first place.

Medical examinations

Many large employers arrange for new staff to attend a medical examination before starting work or, if work has started, make it a condition of employment. The cost is met by the employing company.

Medical questionnaire.

To avoid this expense a new entrant should be asked to complete a medical questionnaire either before or at the start of employment. If the employee is reasonably healthy, this is filed with other personnel records. If any area appears to indicate cause for concern the entry should be checked with the company medical adviser and, if considered necessary, arrangements made for a full medical examination. This procedure saves time and avoids the expense of examining an apparently healthy person. An example of a basic medical questionnaire for this purpose is given on page 133.

Period of settling in.

Induction programme

Starting in a new job can be a daunting process to many and some form

Medical questionnaire. Confidential

Family name .... **Forename(s)** ....

Date of birth ....

Please answer the questions listed below. Depending on the information provided you may be asked to attend for a medical examination by a company doctor.

Have you ever:	Tick if NO	If YES give details
• suffered a serious injury or illness?	☐	
• had an operation?	☐	
• received in-patient hospital treatment?	☐	

Have you in the last five years:		
• resided in hospital for 4 weeks or longer?	☐	
• suffered from any mental illness or stress?	☐	

Do you now:		
• suffer from any prolonged recurring illness or disability?	☐	
• obtain regular treatment for any reason from your doctor?	☐	
• know of any medical facts about yourself that we should be aware of?	☐	

Have you ever suffered from:

• heart, lung, intestine, stomach, skin or other problems? If so give details.

I certify that the above information is correct. I understand that if after my appointment the information given above proves to be false I may be liable to dismissal.

Signed .... **Date** ....

of induction is useful. In a small firm this can be as short as an informal talk by one of the managers but in a larger organisation the procedure can occupy a week. Induction should be seen as a settling-in period where the new employee is not under pressure and where he/she is given time and training to familiarise him/herself with the working organisation.

Advise candidate in advance.

The candidate should be told in advance the form the programme will take and given brief details of its content. It will usually take place from the first day of joining the organisation but in larger firms it may be delayed until a date can be arranged for group attendances.

Subjects covered during induction.

Induction serves to initiate the newcomer to the firm and place of work in all aspects. Some examples of topics that could be included in the programme are:

- An outline of the company, its history, departments and management structure
- The function of the company, its products and/or services. A brief note on the main client base
- Details of the associated departments and personalities who the new employee will come into direct contact with during his/her work
- Health and safety
- A talk on the more important parts of the terms of employment. This should include disciplinary procedures
- Employee welfare, facilities and social amenities
- Reporting procedures in the job itself. For individual new employees, an introduction to line managers and others. Where to go for help and advice. The company's policy for training and promotion.

To be effective a programme of induction training will need to be drawn up carefully. Thought must be given to special circumstances, for instance, school leavers who will probably be entering a working environment for the first time. Different levels of management should be consulted on the content of the programme within their particular domain and asked to suggest suitable staff to instruct. Easily digested descriptive material should be written and produced and handed out at the end of each session.

Written material should support lectures.

Attendance at a course of induction should be entered on the new employee's personal record.

Conclusion

You now await the chosen applicant's acceptance and start date, and responses from the referees provided by the candidate.

Other matters can well wait until the new employee's first day of work, for instance bank details for monthly salary arrangements. You will eventually need a P45 but it can often take a while before it is passed on from the previous employer.

You are now able to sign off the record of recruitment as being successfully completed. You should also make arrangements for the details of the other suitable but unsuccessful candidates to be filed.

The taxing but vital job of recruiting is over and you can now get back to the routine job of running the company.

◀ FURTHER READING FROM KOGAN PAGE ▶

British Qualifications, annual

How To Be a Good Judge of Character: A Practical Guide to Assessing People, D Mackenzie Davey

How to Recruit Good Managers – and How to Keep Them, Robert S Redmond, 1989

How to Write a Staff Manual: A Guide for Managers, S L Brock and S R Cabell, 1989

Keeping the Best: Building a Competitive Workforce, Martin John Yate, 1991

Readymade Business Forms, Michael Armstrong, 1991

Readymade Interview Questions, Malcolm Peel, 1989

Readymade Job Advertisements: A Recruitment Toolkit for Every Manager, Neil Wenborn, 1991

Successful Induction: How To Get the Most From Your New Employees, Judy Skeats, 1991

Talk It Out: 4 Steps to Managing People Problems in Your Organisation, Daniel Dana, 1991

◀ INDEX ▶